The Hidden Yor

This is a guide to the *real* Yorkshire.

Our county has more than its fair share of special places, but many of them are easily overlooked by the casual visitor. *The Hidden Yorkshire* is a unique guide, researched and written by a dedicated team of local people, which aims to ensure that you get the most from your visit.

Whatever your interests, *The Hidden Yorkshire* tells you where to find the very best Yorkshire has to offer. Whether you fancy a walk in the hills or a day at the races, we can tell you where to head for. It's all here: art galleries and angling opportunities, stately homes and romantic gardens, sophisticated boutiques and fascinating craft workshops – together with a definitive guide to the very best pubs, restaurants, hotels and bed & breakfast escapes.

It's easy enough to find your way to the tourist-traps, but it can be very difficult to track down those magical places which make for a really memorable holiday. *The Hidden Yorkshire* will help you to stay ahead of the crowd.

The Boar's Head Hotel

RIPLEY CASTLE ESTATE, HARROGATE HG3 3AY

The Boar's Head is one of the Great Inns of England. This is an Inn with high-quality accommodation, a bar, for locals, as well as visitors to have a pint in, and dining facilities where you don't have to wear a tie or talk in hushed whispers over a sculpture on a plate! We believe that staying with us is an experience, with the emphasis on quality, fun, individuality and informality!

Antique furniture and pictures were brought down from the attics of Ripley Castle when The Boar's Head was opened in 1990, and Lady Ingilby, who has a fine eye for style and detail, created the result. Each bedroom is individually decorated and king-sized beds enable you to lose your partner in the night! Catamarans have been thoughtfully provided in the bathroom so that you can push the boat out during your stay, and satellite TV and mini-bar provide world-wide entertainment and spiritual consolation.

The formal walled gardens are a joy and freely accessible to guests staying at the hotel. Huge herbaceous borders, rose gardens, a fine assembly of tropical plants in the Hot Houses, rare vegetables, thousands of daffodils and narcissi and the National Hyacinth Collection all compete for space! Leave time for a walk around the grounds, lake and deer park - it will give you a healthy appetite for your next delicious meal.

TELEPHONE 01423 771888 FAX 01423 771509

Little Gems

Courtesy of The Blue Lion

There is certainly no shortage of charming accommodation of character in North Yorkshire. The choice ranges from sophisticated hotels to welcoming Dales farmhouses, from 18th century follies to historic coaching inns. Here we give details of places where you can be sure of a memorable stay.

Millgate House, Millgate, Richmond (01748 823571)

This elegant Georgian townhouse and its award-winning terraced garden offer a quiet and relaxed environment literally seconds away from Richmond's historic cobbled square and all the facilities of the town centre. The spacious, comfortable and tastefully-furnished rooms have delightful views over the River Swale and, of course, the garden. The latter is imaginatively planted, and includes a fine selection of Old English roses – making it the perfect place to while away a summer's morning or evening.

Bed and breakfast £25 per person in a double room. Single person supplement of £10.

Lupton Towers Vegetarian Country House, Lupton, Kirby Lonsdale (015395 67400)

Set in open countryside and approached by a private drive, this unusual guest house serves only vegetarian meals.

The bedroom at the top of the Tower has fine views of the open fields, together with a Victorian fireplace for those chilly Yorkshire evenings. The lounge downstairs also has an open fire and fine antique furniture.

Vegetarian evening meals are served in the dining room and the owners will also prepare packed lunches for their guests.

Prices range from £28 per person in a double room with breakfast, to £56 for the double at the top of the Tower.

The Old Hall Guest House, Bellerby, Leyburn (01969 623028)

This historic 16th Century house stands at the centre of the village of Bellerby. It is believed to have an ancient tunnel that leads to the local Manor House and the East wing of the house was burnt down by Cromwell's men as they searched for Royalists.

The guest house has two large and very comfortable double bedrooms, one of which still contains a Priest's Hole, now converted into a lavatory.

Bed and breakfast prices start at £18 per person with a single person supplement of £5. Evening meals can be ordered in advance (three courses with coffee £9).

School House, Coxwold, near York (01347 868356)

Set in the scenic village of Coxwold to the North of York, this charming floral cottage has three bedrooms available for guests. As befits a cottage built in the 17th Century, the furnishings are in period style. The three bedrooms are all well appointed and two have an adjoining bathroom.

Evening meals are available, and since there is no alcohol license, guests are welcome to bring their own wine. Guests will also be interested in author Laurence Sterne's former residence, Shandy Hall, which stands nearby.

Meals are home-cooked and ham and eggs for breakfast and cream teas in the afternoon are both popular choices.

Prices for bed and breakfast start at £17 per person sharing a double room.

The Holly Tree, East Witton, Wensleydale (01969 622383)

This is said to be one of the oldest houses in the Yorkshire Dales and was built in the 13th Century as a stud farm. The white-washed house stands in the pretty village of East Witton in the heart of Wensleydale.

The food from the award-winning chef centres on local produce such as pheasant, cheese and venison.

There are two double and two twin bedrooms. Bed and breakfast prices start at £35 per person including a five course dinner.

The Old Vicarage, Easingwold, York (01347 821015)

Those in search of the English idyll will certainly enjoy this delightful Georgian country house set right in the market place of the village of Easingwold near York. In the grounds there is a croquet lawn and a beautiful walled rose garden.

Until the turn of the century, the house was a vicarage and the bedrooms are suitably quiet and comfortable. Evening meals can be taken at 'Truffles' or at the George pub, both a short walk away in the village.

There are six bedrooms (two doubles, two twins and two singles) and all have either a shower or bath attached. Prices start at £21 per person for bed and breakfast (deluxe £25; single £25).

Croft Farm, Fylingthorpe, near Whitby (01947 880231)

Panoramic views of the moors and Robin Hood's Bay and a farmhouse breakfast of fresh eggs and milk await visitors to this lovely old farmhouse on the edge of Fylingthorpe near Whitby.

Typically for a Yorkshire farmhouse, it is well equipped with fireplaces throughout and there is a very cosy atmosphere. Excellent lunchtime and evening meals can be found at the Fylingdales Inn in the village.

Bedrooms include a double with bathroom and a large family room. Bed and

breakfast prices start at £17 and there is also a self-contained cottage available.

Hetherdene Hotel, Goathland (01947 896334)

Fans of the television programme *Heartbeat* will find this quiet turn-of-the-century hotel an ideal place to stay. The hotel, stands in an expanse of open moorland outside the village of Goathland on top of the North York Moors. Many of the seven large bedrooms have attached bathrooms, one room is ensuite and all rooms have TVs and log fires.

The hotel is traditionally furnished throughout and guests can relax with a fireside drink in the lounge. The home cooked meals are much praised and vegetarians are well catered for.

Prices for bed and breakfast range from £55 for a double room and £40 for a single.

Brandymires Guest House, Hawes (01969 667482)

Situated on the outskirts of this bustling market town in the Dales, Brandymires offers some perfect views of Wensleydale from each of its four elegant double bedrooms. Two of the bedrooms have four-poster beds and all have their own seating area.

The excellent cooking has a local flavour, and wild game and Yorkshire meats feature prominently on the menu. After dinner, guests can retire to the bar for a quiet drink or explore the bustling pubs of Hawes.

Bed and breakfast is £18 per person and there is single person supplement of £8.

Hammer and Hand Country Guest House, Hutton le Hole (01751 417300)

Built in 1748 as the local beer house, this listed property of character now provides bed and breakfast in a traditional Yorkshire setting. The stone house, which is set in a pretty garden, faces onto the village green.

It is full of period features and there are three cruck-beamed double bedrooms. Stone fireplaces and panel doors abound throughout (even the showers are beamed). Guests can enjoy home-cooked meals by candlelight or relax by the inglenook fireplace in the lounge.

Prices for bed and breakfast start at £18 per person.

Waterford House, Middleham, Wensleydale (01969 622090)

Overlooking Middleham's market square, Waterford House provides its guests with a real taste of luxury right on the edge of the Dales National Park.

The five bedrooms all have ensuite bathrooms, and each is supplied with coffee, fresh fruit and a TV. Two of the bedrooms have four-poster beds and oak beams.

Dinner can be eaten either in the traditional 17th Century oak dining room or in the Regency style dining room. There is an extensive menu of local dishes and the wine list contains over a thousand fine wines from around the World.

A four course table d'hôte meal costs from around £19.50, à la carte is also available.

The drawing room boasts a baby grand piano which guests may play. Bed and breakfast from £32.50 per person (£7.50 single person supplement).

Ivy Dene Country Guest House, West Witton, Leyburn (01969 622785)

A lovely listed three hundred year old farmhouse set in the Dales National Park. There are five double bedrooms, one of which has a four-poster bed.

Downstairs there is a popular bar in the oak-beamed lounge with an open fire. The house is particularly well situated for touring and walking.

A three course home-cooked evening meal is available from £12.50, and traditional desserts such as bread and butter pudding and sticky toffee pudding are favourites.
Bed and breakfast from £22 per person (two nights minimum stay).

The Pigsty, Robin Hood's Bay
(Landmark Trust 01628 825925)
Complete with Doric columns, this former pigsty was built in the 1880s by local landowner Squire Barry. It has now been lovingly converted into a comfortable one-bedroom cottage by the Landmark Trust.

Inspired by classical Mediterranean architecture, the Pigsty affords its guests some spectacular views of Robin Hood's Bay from the front windows. Those worried about the lingering odour from its original inhabitants will be pleased to learn that it has not been used as a sty for several decades.
Prices range from £194 for a four night stay in winter to £611 per week in mid summer.

Culloden Tower, Richmond
(Landmark Trust 01628 825925)
Set in the parkland of a long-since demolished house, Culloden Tower was built in 1746 by John Yorke, MP for Richmond, to mark the final establishment of Hanoverian rule.

The Tower has two large octagonal bedrooms, the lower with Gothic carvings and plasterwork, the upper with a truly wonderful ceiling decorated in Classical style. The arch windows look down a steep slope towards the River Swale below. The town of Richmond is only a few hundred yards away.
The price for four people ranges from £267 for four nights in winter to £734 for a week in mid-summer.

The Grammar School, Kirby Hill
(Landmark Trust 01628 825925)
Those in search of a scholastic connection will be delighted with the Master's Tudor lodgings at the centre of this ancient Grammar School. The lodgings boast a large library of old school books and the main bedroom has fine views over the churchyard and the village green of Kirby Hill.

The school was founded in 1556 and the wardens of the Trust were chosen by a curious method. On the Feast of the Decollation of St John, parishioners were invited to write their names on pieces of paper which were then encased in small balls of wax and stored in a jar of water. Two balls of wax were then selected and the rest left in the jar until vacancies arose. The jar and remaining wax balls can still be seen in the school today.
The flat has two bedrooms, and prices for four guests range from £204 for four nights in winter to £603 in high summer.

Cawood Castle
(Landmark Trust 01628 825925)
The Gatehouse is all that remains of the original 15th century Cawood Castle, which stands in the quiet town of Cawood by the River Ouse. Accommodation is in two spacious rooms and the living room has bay windows at each end giving wonderful views of the town.

Guests to Cawood Castle will be in good company because there is a long and illustrious list of historic visitors including Henry VIII, Edward I and Cardinal Wolsey.
The Gatehouse has only one bedroom which sleeps three guests. Prices range from £178 for four nights in winter to £485 for a week in high summer.

A celebration weekend coming up or do you just want to get away and relax?

Take a certain style, add more than a hint of comfort and renowned and award-winning food, both, in The Restaurant and the ever popular Cricketers Bistro - you are set for a weekend to remember.

With the North York Moors, Castle Howard and Rievaulx only short distances away there is plenty to discover. With a lovely garden, a bottle of champagne and a bowl of strawberries, or a real log fire, traditional tea and a good book - there is plenty of reason not to.

To find out more about special events and breaks, please telephone us on 01653 628234

The Worsley Arms Hotel, Hovingham,
North Yorkshire YO6 4LA

AA ★★★ ❀❀ The Good Hotel Guide ETB ♛♛♛♛ Highly Commended
Partners Euan and Debbi Rodger

Stay in the heart of York in the former residence of the Assize Court Judges dating from the early 1700s.

This family-owned hotel offers top class accommodation and personal service which is second to none.

ETB 4 CROWNS
HIGHLY COMMENDED

◆ GOURMET RESTAURANT ◆
◆ SHORT BREAKS AVAILABLE ◆
◆ MINSTER VIEWS ◆

9 Lendal, York YO1 2AQ
Tel: (01904) 638733
Fax: (01904) 679947

Beamsley Hospital, near Skipton (Landmark Trust 01628 825925)

This unusual circular Alms House features a very intriguing layout. Guests must cross a small chapel at the centre of the building each time they pass between its oddly shaped rooms. It was built in 1593 by the Countess of Cumberland and the curious shape was intended to reflect the six circles on her husband's coat of arms.

Until recently the hospital, situated behind a row of small roadside houses, was inhabited by a small community of nuns. In its present incarnation the Alms House sleeps five guests in its three bedrooms.

Prices for 5 people range from £549 up to £912 for a week.

George & Dragon Hotel, Kirkbymoorside (01751 433334)

A coaching inn since the seventeenth century, this hotel is set at the centre of the old market town of Kirkbymoorside. For three hundred years the George and Dragon has been the ideal stopping place for travellers en route from the Great North Road (now the A1) to the East Coast.

Three qualified chefs offer a variety of home-cooked meals in the bar and the candle-lit dining room. There are also over a hundred wines available, all carefully chosen by the owner Stephen Colling, whose five years as a wine merchant were clearly well spent.

Spread across two buildings to the rear of the hotel, one of which is an old Rectory, the nineteen bedrooms are imaginatively decorated and many have either four-poster beds or beautifully draped bed heads. All have televisions and direct-dial telephones.

£79 for a double room including breakfast.

Simonstone Hall, Hawes (01969 667255)

Simonstone Hall is a former hunting lodge and stands one and a half miles north of Hawes on the road to Muker and The Buttertubs. A gracious country house, this is the perfect base for the guided walking and shooting weekends on offer in the surrounding Wensleydale countryside.

The house has been lovingly restored with antiques and many of the eighteen bedrooms have glorious and unspoilt views of Stags Fell and Upper Wensleydale. The Superior Dales Rooms are two-room suites furnished with French sleigh beds and four-posters.

The emphasis is very much on tranquillity, elegance and good food and wine. Fine cuisine from the award-winning new head chef is always on offer in the dining room.

Prices range from £45 for bed and breakfast only, in a Dales Room, to £77 per person for dinner, bed and breakfast, staying in a Superior Dales Room. Special midweek breaks are also on offer.

King's Arms, Askrigg (01969 650258)

The King's Arms is a Georgian manor house and former racing stables set at the centre of the small town of Askrigg. A stone's throw from the hotel there are two waterfalls, Mill Gill and Whitfield Gill (Mill Gill was captured on canvas by the artist Turner during his visit to the town).

Guests can choose from three eating areas, the Silks' Room Grill, the Clubroom Restaurant and, for a less formal atmosphere, the Drovers bars. The excellent cuisine has earned the King's Arms two rosettes in the AA Best Restaurant guide and the chef has collected no fewer than seven national food awards.

There are eleven double bedrooms and all have ensuite bathrooms. The best of country house features together with the inside of a Dales pub.

Double rooms £45 per person (single person supplement £10) including breakfast.

The White House, Harrogate (01423 501388)

Set on The Stray (a parkland of 200 acres that surrounds the town of Harrogate) The White House is only an eight minute walk from the town centre. The house was originally built for the mayor of Harrogate in 1836 as a copy of a Venetian Villa.

Although the house has eight double rooms and two singles, it has more of a feel of a private home than a hotel, with books and games on tables and roaring fires in the grate. It has two AA rosettes for cuisine. The menu changes seasonally and in winter you may find Smoked baby haggis with neeps and a whisky cream sauce as a starter with pan-fried Ostrich in orange and cranberry sauce.

A double room is from £47.50 per person for bed and breakfast (£68.50 single). Luxury breaks are regularly on offer such as the two-night stay at £67.50 per person including the a la carte dinner.

Hob Green Country House, Markington, Harrogate (01423 770031)

This small and quiet country house hotel is run by the Hutchinson family, who share it as their home. Set in 800 acres of rolling park land near the pretty village of Markington, the house was built in the early 18th century, though parts are even older.

There are twelve bedrooms, all uniquely and carefully furnished with antiques. Evening meals can be taken in the restaurant at the rear of the house which has some spectacular views across the valley.

Prices for a double room including full English breakfast from £90 for two people.

Ripon Spa, Ripon (01765 602172)

Ripon Spa is every inch the grand Edwardian hotel. Family-run for more than 80 years, the hotel is beautifully set in award winning gardens. The hotel also boasts one of the largest croquet clubs in the North of England, and guests may choose from a number of lawns.

There are forty rooms and prices vary according to size and time of stay. The hotel nurtures close ties with Ripon Races and this is evident in the Turf Tavern where excellent traditional English meals are available evenings and lunch times.

Price for a double room from £75 including breakfast.

Judge's Lodgings, York (01904 638733)

This Grade I listed building is situated in the very centre of the old town of York. Built in 1710 the building was in private ownership until 1806, when it became the residence of visiting judges on the Court of Assizes.

In 1979 the lodgings were carefully converted into a small hotel with 14 rooms. All are individually decorated and the most impressive has a king-size four-poster bed and a sunken bath.

The Brasserie Restaurant has a full à la carte menu, whilst for a lighter meal, the bar also serves a variety of hot and cold snacks.

Prices for bed and breakfast start at £95 for two people sharing a double room.

Green Dragon Inn & Hotel, Hardraw, Hawes (01969 667392)

Guests at this hotel will find Hardraw Force, at 98 feet the highest single drop waterfall in Britain just outside the window. Also, every year, on the second Sunday in September, the Hardraw Brass Band contest is held in the grounds.

The Inn dates from the early 16th century and the quality of hospitality is excellent. Theakston's ales and delicious snacks are served in the bar, whilst the modern hotel's 16 rooms provide total comfort.
Prices for bed and breakfast start at £22 per person per night.

Harefield Hall, Pateley Bridge (01423 711429)

This 300 year old hall was built as a monastery in the reign of Henry VIII and now provides a delightful retreat even for guests of a less holy disposition.

There is a complete leisure centre with steam baths, tennis courts, sauna, three gymnasiums and a swimming pool. Fishing is also available on a private 3/4 mile stretch of the River Nidd. The hotel has 15 bedrooms (13 doubles and 2 singles).

There is a full à la carte menu in the restaurant and the bar serves only home cooked food. In the wall of the restaurant there is the skull of a poacher. He is said to have been shot by an angry Lord of the Manor with whose daughters he was conducting simultaneous affairs!
Prices for bed and breakfast start at £37 per person, rising to £67 for a double room with four poster bed.

The Parsonage, Escrick, York (01904 728111)

The Parsonage is rich in history. Records show it to have been passed between several different families and baronies since the 11th century.

Now, surrounded by formal gardens and woodland, it is a magnificent ivy covered country house hotel.

All of the 13 bedrooms have ensuite bathrooms and there are several living rooms in which guests can relax and enjoy a quiet drink. Cuisine in the large restaurant is Anglo-French and uses only the best of local ingredients.
Prices for a double room with four-poster bed with Full English Breakfast £125 (two sharing). Three Day Breaks £50 per person per night.

The Tontine, near Northallerton (01609 882671)

A perfect stage-post for walkers, this country house stands at the very start of the Cleveland Way. It was originally built as a turnpike in 1804, but this role was quickly cut short by the advent of the railways. The name Tontine actually refers to a curious insurance practice adopted by the owners whereby the last member of the consortium to stay alive sweeps the pool of premiums.

The house is rumoured to be haunted, though the McCoys who have lived here since 1976 have yet to see a ghost. Haunted or not, the house is certainly unusual. One Norwegian owner kept her hats in a coffin. The Hotel won the 1989 'Utterly Acceptable Mild Eccentricity Award'.
There are six bedrooms and prices for bed and breakfast start at £99 for two people sharing a double room.

Grants Hotel, Harrogate (01423 560666)

This Victorian hotel is situated at the very heart of Harrogate. As a base for exploring the shops and restaurants of this busy spa town, Grants Hotel has few equals.

There are 42 lavishly furnished bedrooms. For the more energetic, the hotel boasts a fully-equipped leisure complex with sauna, steambath, Jacuzzi, gym and tennis court. And, to put all those lost calories back on, an excellent range of fine food and drink is available at the hotel's Chimney Pots Restaurant and Bar.
Prices for bed and breakfast start at £94.50.

Chapters

Restaurant & Hotel

27 High Street, Stokesley, Cleveland
Tel: 01642 711888 Fax: 01642 713387

A former 18th century coaching inn,. situated in the centre of Stokesley, a picturesque market town.

Restaurant and Bistro are Good Food Guide, Egon Ronay and Michelin recommended. The popular bistro offers a fun, relaxed atmosphere, whereas the more formal restaurant is perfect for special occasions.

A wide and varied menu using top quality produce. Favourite dishes include fresh fishcakes with a curry malibu sauce, duck stuffed with spinach and an irresistible creme brulee with kirsch and cherries.

---

13 ensuite bedrooms

TARIFF

Bed & Full English Breakfast
From £50.00 per night

Special Weekend Rates available

SET AMONGST 3 ACRES OF BEAUTIFULLY LANDSCAPED GARDENS, WITHIN WALKING DISTANCE OF THE CENTRE OF PICKERING, RYEDALE'S FINEST HOTEL AND BISTRO OFFERS THE PERFECT SETTING FOR BUSINESS AND SOCIAL ENTERTAINING, WEDDINGS AND PRIVATE FUNCTIONS.

EIGHT LUXURY ENSUITE BEDROOMS.

AWARD-WINNING CUISINE IN THE BISTRO, A WIDE SELECTION OF MENUS FROM ACROSS EUROPE TO DELIGHT THE MOST DISCERNING PALETTE. LUNCHES AND DINNERS SERVED DAILY IN THE CONSERVATORY

The Lodge, Middleton Road, Pickering, North Yorkshire
Tel: 01751 472976
Fax: 01751 476852

Devonshire Arms, Bolton Abbey, Skipton (01756 710441)

This 17th century former coaching inn is at the heart of the Bolton Abbey estate, which is owned by the Duke of Devonshire. Bolton Abbey and the beautiful scenery that surrounds it will provide ample opportunity for exploring. The adjacent Devonshire Club has a swimming pool and full sporting facilities.

Outside the hotel there is an Italian Garden and the hotel's vast grounds lead right down to the River Wharfe. Inside, there is a lively bar and superb meals are available at the Burlington Restaurant, which was recently awarded two red rosettes for its fine cooking.

There are 41 bedrooms and prices range from £150 to £250 for two people sharing a double room with full breakfast.

Worsley Arms, Hovingham, Malton (01653 628234)

Wealthy local landowner William Worsley built the Worsley Arms in 1840 to house some of his many guests. Now the perfect country house, it is located opposite the village green at the centre of Hovingham. The attractions of Castle Howard are only five miles away and the village is on the edge of the North York Moors.

The Worsley Arms combines the atmosphere of a village pub with comforts of a fully-equipped country hotel. Open fires are lit all year round. There are 18 bedrooms, ten in the main house and eight in converted cottages on the green.

Prices range from £75 (single) to £115 (double) for Bed and Breakfast.

The Boar's Head, Ripley (01423 771888)

Built in the shadow of Ripley Castle, the Boar's Head was originally called the Star Inn. It was a coaching house during the 19th Century and welcomed travellers from the Leeds to Edinburgh coach every weekday. When the inn was ordered to close on Sundays in 1919 by the religious Sir William Ingilby, the village of Ripley was left 'dry' for more than seventy years.

Fortunately, the present occupant of Ripley Castle, Sir Thomas Ingilby, had the good sense to re-open the inn and there are 25 luxurious bedrooms. The hotel is decorated throughout with paintings and furnishings from the 660 year old Ripley Castle itself.

The freshest of seasonal foods are served daily in the restaurant and there is an extensive wine list personally chosen by Sir Thomas and a fine selection of malt whiskies.

Bed & Breakfast prices start from £85 (single) to £98 (double).

East Ayton Lodge, Moor Lane, East Ayton, near Scarborough (01723 864227)

A family-owned hotel and restaurant set in three acres of tranquil grounds near the Derwent, East Ayton Lodge offers convenient access to the attractions of Scarborough and the eastern parts of the North Yorkshire Moors National Park.

The rooms, two of which feature traditional four-poster beds, are furnished to a high standard and include all the conveniences and comforts you would expect – together with one or two little extras. The restaurant specialises in English, French and vegetarian cuisine, complemented by an extensive and interesting wine list. There is also a well-stocked and cosy bar.

Bed and Breakfast starts at £65 per couple. All rooms are double or twin; single person supplement payable.

Sponsored by Ogden the Jeweller of Harrogate.

ASENBY, THIRSK, NORTH YORKSHIRE.

01845 577286 (fax. 577109)

Table Talk

Yorkshire has a remarkable variety of good places to eat - ranging from the impeccably traditional cuisine of secluded country hotels to the airy and easygoing atmosphere of up-to-the-minute bistros. We have selected the most outstanding in one way or another. Do remember that booking is often advisable, and sometimes essential. And do ensure that you confirm details of opening times and prices before making a special journey.

Of the northernmost Dales, Wensleydale is particularly well-provided with opportunities for a memorable meal. **The Rowan Tree (tel. (01969) 650536)** at Askrigg is a small, family-run restaurant set back from the town's main street in its own arched courtyard. Chef, Derek Wylie,

Alex 97
The Friar's Head...at Akebar
could easily become a habit
for good food and wine
Wensleydale, North Yorkshire
Tel: 01677 450201/450591

has an excellent sense of how to combine tastes and textures for maximum effect, and his wife, Pia, provides friendly and unobtrusive service. They offer good value for money at £20 a head for three courses, cheeseboard and coffee. The Rowan Tree's wine list contains a good choice of French and New World wines, informatively characterised and moderately priced.

Another essential stop in Askrigg is **The King's Arms (tel. (01969) 650258)**, a substantial inn which many will recognise as "The Drover's Arms" in the BBC TV series All Creatures Great and Small. Downstairs you will find three bars and the Silks' Room, where you can enjoy a three-course meal in an informal atmosphere for around £15. Upstairs is the comfortable Clubroom Restaurant where a fixed-price à la carte menu at £25 gives you four courses, coffee and home-made sweets. The emphasis is on traditional English cuisine, but inspiration has also been drawn from continental and even oriental sources. There is a good wine list, majoring on reliable wines of proven quality.

Even further up Wensleydale, near Hawes, stands the imposing **Simonstone Hall (tel. (01969) 667255)**, an exuberantly Victorian shooting lodge which now houses a newly-refurbished country house hotel. Food is available to non-residents seven days a week. Three courses in the restaurant will cost around £20, or you can eat in the more informal surroundings of the bar for £14 or so. The restaurant offers a good selection of traditional English game-based dishes, recalling the original function of the building. The bar menu is a little more broadly based, with various continental and international influences making their presence felt.

At the lower end of Wensleydale, just south of Leyburn, lies Middleham, a racing town with a distinctly cosmopolitan feel. This is reflected in the varied and imaginative menus offered by **The White Swan Hotel (tel. (01969) 622093)** in the Market Place. Energetic proprietor, Chris Wager, aided by her talented head chef, has made this cosy coaching inn a place to enjoy top-quality food in an easygoing, informal atmosphere. Three courses from the à la carte menu should cost you less than £20, and set meals are available from Tuesday to Thursday for around half this price. Try the citrus tart if you're fortunate enough to find it on offer.

Less than two miles south on the A6108 is **The Blue Lion (tel. (01969) 624273)** at East Witton. Another one-time shooting lodge, the inn has a longstanding reputation for providing excellent food and was 1994's Dining Pub of the Year. It has two bar areas, and two pleasantly-proportioned and intimate dining rooms. For around £20 you can choose three courses à la carte from a menu which offers modern English cuisine with some exciting Continental twists. The wine-list is well-judged, with an emphasis on New World, French and Italian vineyards. The atmosphere is relaxing, service is good-humoured, and the presentation of the food is excellent.

Masham is a few miles further down the Ure. Just off its huge square, in Silver Street, you can find **The Floodlite (tel. (01765) 689000)**, a small restaurant with a strong local following opened by chef Charles Flood and his wife eleven years ago. The Floodlite is open for lunch from

Friday to Sunday, and for dinner from Tuesday to Saturday. Three courses in the evening will cost around £20, and you can consume a good three-course lunch in an undemanding atmosphere for £10.50. Menus are particularly strong on game and fish.

Returning to Leyburn and heading due east on the A684 towards Bedale soon brings you to **The Friar's Head (tel. (01677 450201)** at Akebar, just beyond Constable Burton. Here you can eat in the bar or the 'Cloisters', a plant-packed conservatory with a massive stone table at its centre. For a modest £15 you can choose three courses from an inventive menu seven days a week. Presentation is often imaginative, and the desserts are particularly noteworthy. There are plenty of options for vegetarians, and the service is pleasant and helpful.

The Foresters Arms (tel. (01969) 640272) at Carlton, the main town in Coverdale, is a well-respected inn, whose quality is backed up by a host of awards and commendations. It dates back to the 1640s, and its stone-flagged floors and oak beams give it masses of genuine Dales character. The food is modern, British in style, with a special emphasis on fresh fish and game in season. Around sixty wines are listed, mainly French and New World. Food is served throughout the week, excepting Sunday evenings and Mondays.

The Buck (tel. (01756) 760228) at Buckden, in the imposing surroundings of Upper Wharfedale, is a 16th century coaching inn which was once the meeting place for the local stag-hunt. It has received a variety of plaudits, including the award of an AA rosette for four consecutive years. The cuisine is English in style, with a dash of Continental influence – try their braised shoulder of lamb in filo pastry if it happens to be available. A bar meal costs around £15 for three courses, and there is a separate restaurant open in the evenings with a set price menu at £22.95 which includes three courses and coffee.

Heading south down Wharfedale and taking the B6265 towards Skipton leads you to the village of Hetton. Here you can find **The Angel (tel. (01756) 730263)**, an unspoiled drover's pub with all the quirky charm that a building begun 400 years ago inevitably accumulates. The restaurant offers a fixed-price menu at £26.50 for four courses and coffee, or you can select three courses in the bar-brasserie for around £13. Food is a lively mix of English, French and Italian. There is an impressive list of some 250 wines, mainly French. The maximum mark-up is very moderate, which means that the better wines represent particularly good value. The Angel was Egon Ronay Pub of the Year in 1995.

Moving on to Skipton, **Le Caveau (tel. (01756) 794274)** at 86 High Street was originally the town gaol. From Tuesday to Saturday you can sit beneath its splendid stone-vaulted ceilings and enjoy a very moderately-priced lunch or choose three courses à la carte for around £17. The food on offer is traditional English cuisine with a hint of French, and there is a special emphasis on fish. Portions are generous and well-presented, and it is easy enough to see why Le Caveau won its AA rosette. The wine list runs to thirty or so wines, with a good selection of half-bottles.

Also in Skipton, **Napier's (tel. (01756) 799688)** on Chapel Hill is a lively restaurant in a cosy 17th century building which incorporates remains from four centuries earlier. Ian Ackroyd, the proprietor, is a motor-sports enthusiast, as will be clear from the masses of racing memorabilia on show. The main menu and the large specials board cover a wide range, including pasta, seafood and a good selection of appealing vegetarian dishes – vegans are also catered for. Three courses will cost around £16. There is a comprehensive wine list, strong on New World wines, and moderately priced.

Heading north-west from Skipton on the A65 brings you to Giggleswick, just south-west of which you can find **The Old Station Free House (tel. (01729) 823623)** in Brackenber Lane. Here you can enjoy three courses of good value, unpretentious home-cooked food for around £10 in the dining room or the bar. If you fancy a post-lunch stroll, why not take advantage of a variety of pleasant circuits on the opposite side of the railway line.

The Devonshire Arms (tel. (01756) 710441) at Bolton Abbey, on the A59 north-east of Skipton, is a country house hotel in the grand style, furnished with antiques and effects from Chatsworth, seat of the Duke and Duchess of Devonshire. The food in the Burlington restaurant is unquestionably superb, although the atmosphere of pomp and circumstance can be somewhat oppressive. The three-course table d'hôte is priced at £37.00, the food is classic modern English cuisine, and the wine list is just as you would expect it to be. The Devonshire Arms is County Restaurant of the Year 1997.

Still further down Wharfedale, at Pool, between Otley and Bramhope, is **Monkman's Bistro (tel. (0113) 2841105)**. Set in a Georgian House, its five interconnecting rooms can seat up to 120 in a modern, up-tempo atmosphere. The menu makes exciting reading, with lots of interesting combinations inspired by – amongst others – southern European and Far-Eastern cuisines. Expect to pay around £20 for three courses. The wine list is equally engaging, and there is also a generous and tempting selection of malt whiskies.

As you would expect, there is a good choice of places to dine in Harrogate. **The Drum and Monkey (tel. (01423) 502650)** at 5 Montpellier Gardens is always busy, and if you don't book the chances are that you will have to queue. The establishment specialises exclusively in fresh fish – pretty much anything you can imagine that happens to be in season. Presentation is simple and unpretentious, portions are generous. Three courses will cost about £18. The atmosphere, especially in the bar downstairs, is lively and the staff are genuinely friendly.

The White House (tel. (01423) 501388) at 10 Park Parade is an imposing copy of a Venetian villa built in 1836 as a private residence for the then Mayor of Harrogate. It is furnished with antiques and retains very much the feel of a private house. The frequently-changed menu is centred around fresh seasonal produce, and the dishes are modern English in style. Three courses will cost £25 or so. Winner of the Which County Hotel of the Year award in 1995, The White House is closed on Sundays except by arrangement, and booking for lunch is essential.

Betty's Cafeteria (tel. (01423) 502746) at 1 Parliament Street is very much a Yorkshire institution – or at least an institution amongst visitors to Yorkshire. There can be no disputing the quality of their teas and light meals, which are available until mid-evening. This said, you certainly pay through the nose for the privilege of being served by waitresses in pseudo-Dickensian costume. For some obscure reason, everything that appears on the table seems to come with its own doily. The Betty's empire also has outposts at St Helen's Square in York, 188 High Street in Northallerton and The Grove, Ilkley. Even if you don't eat there, take a look at their excellent cakes and chocolates – they make much-appreciated presents for folk back home.

Not too far from Harrogate, at Low Laithe on the B6165 between Ripley and Pateley Bridge, is **The Dusty Miller Restaurant (tel. (01423) 780837)**. Sited in a solid, stone-built house it offers classic English and French cuisine in a cosy and comfortable atmosphere. There is a set dinner for £24 which offers three courses and some of those little extras which add so much to one's enjoyment. Alternatively you can choose three courses à la carte for around £28. Ideal for recharging your batteries after a show in town is the late dinner menu served until 11pm. It consists of a light, interesting main course with, again, one or two little extras. The Dusty Miller is open from Tuesday to Saturday, evenings only (other times by arrangement).

On the A61 Harrogate to Ripon road you can find **The Boar's Head Hotel (tel. (01423) 771888)**, part of the Ripley Castle Estate. It is open for lunch and dinner seven days a week, offering modern English cuisine cleverly enhanced with Mediterranean flavours. There is a choice of two fixed-price three-course menus (at £27.50 and £30), or you can opt for the six course 'menu gourmand' at £30. There is also a popular bar/bistro where you can expect to pay £15 or so for a three-course evening meal. There is plenty of atmosphere in this old coaching inn, and the staff manage to hit the right balance between friendliness and professionalism.

The Muse Cafe (tel. (01937) 580201) at 16 Bank Street in the centre of Wetherby is a light and airy new brasserie/bistro with a Mediterranean look and a go-ahead atmosphere. The extensive blackboard menu offers a wide range of dishes made to order, including fish, game, pastas and salads – definitely something for everyone here. A three-course meal will cost around £15, but there are plenty of lighter options, including a popular tapas selection. House wines start at £8.95. The Muse Cafe is closed on Sundays and Mondays, open other days from 10.30am to 9.30pm.

The Wine Exchange (tel. (01937) 843188) at 146 High Street, Boston Spa, just south of Wetherby, is a wine shop with a lively winebar-cum-bistro seven days a week in the cellar beneath. The atmosphere is lively and informal. You can take a light lunch or choose à la carte for around £15 for three courses. The menu has a generally continental feel about it, which is hardly surprising given that the chef is Swiss. As might be expected, there is an extensive wine list – it covers some fifty different wines – with house wines starting at well under a tenner.

Ripon is notoriously congested in the summer months, but it is well worth fighting your way through its bustling streets to find peace and tranquillity at **The Old Deanery (tel. (01765) 603518)** in Minster Road. This splendid Jacobean mansion, complete with original oak staircase in the entrance hall, includes a wood-panelled lounge and two graceful dining rooms. Here you can enjoy classic French cuisine with a British angle. A three-course evening meal, along with various little extras, will cost you around £30. The table d'hôte at £20 offers the possibility of a stylish, good-value lunch.

York is even more frenetic than Ripon, but **The Blake Head Cafe (tel. (01904) 623767)** at 104 Micklegate is sufficiently well-concealed to avoid being besieged by tourists. Set behind the Blake Head Bookshop, it is a light and airy conservatory with its own specially-designed ash furniture and exhibitions of work by local artists on the walls. It serves a variety of vegetarian meals and snacks from mid-morning to late afternoon daily, including Sundays. Vegan options are always available, and the irresistible cakes – including gluten-free ones – are all baked on the premises. A three-course lunch will cost you around £8. Drinks on offer include organic wines and a changing selection of freshly-squeezed juices.

If you fancy something a little grander, try **The Judges Lodging (tel. (01904) 638733)** at 9 Lendal. This imposing and elaborate Grade 1 listed building was once the official residence of York's Assize court judges. There is an extensive bar meal menu available at lunchtimes and early evenings in the bar, or you can opt for something a little more formal in the restaurant. Table d'hôte menus are available at £11.70 and £14.95, or you can choose three courses à la carte for around £21. The cuisine is British with a variety of Continental influences, and there is an extensive vegetarian menu. The wine list is wide-ranging, with French, Spanish and New World examples.

Heading north on the A1 brings us to Boroughbridge, where you can find **The Black Bull (tel. (01423) 322413)** at 6 St James Square. This traditional hostelry dates back to the 13th century, and its restaurant is set in an elegant and sympathetic extension built using reclaimed brick and timber from the original stables. Chef John Dalby offers a best-of-British menu with the emphasis on fresh local ingredients. Expect to pay around £15 for a three-course meal. The wine list runs to nearly 50 wines, ten of which are available by the glass, and all of which are very moderately priced. Food is served lunchtimes and evenings seven days a week.

As the name suggests, **The Crab and Lobster (tel. (01845) 577286)** in the hamlet of Asenby on the A168 between Dishforth and Thirsk, specialises in seafood. Crockery and tablecloths are decorated with their own tiny crab and lobster images, a straw crab and a straw lobster stalk the thatch on the roof outside. The internal decor is a glorious and unruly jumble of nostalgia-inducing junk, amongst which you can enjoy stylish food at any time of the week except Sunday evenings. A three course meal in the restaurant will cost you £30-£35, or around £20 if you stay in the bar. The fish club sandwich, virtually a meal in itself, makes a very satisfying snack.

Further north still, on the A19 some seven miles north-east of Northallerton, stands a very grand early 19th century building, the Cleveland Tontine Inn. Here you can find **McCoy's at the Tontine (tel. (01609) 882671)**. McCoy's Restaurant is open on Thursday, Friday and Saturday evenings only, but the bistro serves lunch and dinner seven days a week. The restaurant is done out in a bright, 1930s style. A three-course à la carte meal here will cost around £27. The bistro downstairs is low-ceilinged, lively, and marginally less expensive. Both offer a typically French-style menu, carefully prepared and well-presented.

The Black Bull (tel. (01325) 377289) at Moulton, just to the west of the A1 near Richmond, offers, amongst other delights, the chance to take a meal in one of the original Pullman carriages from the Brighton Belle. There are a number of other dining areas, including an attractive conservatory. The menu consists strongly of seafood, although there is a variety of meat dishes for those who are not convinced. Standards are high, and The Black Bull inspires almost fanatical devotion amongst certain sections of the Richmond cognoscenti. Expect to pay around £25 for three courses. Lunches are excellent value at £14.95. Food not available on Sundays.

Darlington, it has to be admitted, is not in Yorkshire. but **The Imperial Express Cafe (tel. (01325) 383297)** at 2 Northumberland Street is well worth bending the rules for. A bustling Italian cafe with a smart black-and-white décor, it offers a variety of specially-imported Italian delicacies and some truly excellent coffee. Booking is essential if you want an evening meal, and last orders are at 8.30pm. A three-course dinner. presented with flair, will cost around £13. Because the cafe goes hand-in-hand with an off-license there is a choice of 175 wines to enjoy with your food, including a very good Amarone – all at off-license prices plus a mere £4 supplement.

Heading west out of Darlington on the A167 will bring you to the dignified town of Yarm. Here, at 104 High Street, you will find **DP Chadwick's (tel. (01642) 888010)**, a light, bright bistro open Tuesday to Saturday, 11.30am to 9.30pm. It has the kind of varied internationalist menu which you would expect, with a mass of blackboard specials. A three-course lunch will cost you £15 or so, a three-course evening feed around £20. The sparky atmosphere draws customers from far and wide. Since it isn't possible to book, you should be sure to arrive in good time.

Proximity to Teesside seems to encourage the flourishing of lively, modern eateries. **Chapters (tel. (01642) 711888)**, at 27 High Street in Stokesley, is a well-known bistro and restaurant set in an 18th century coaching inn. The décor is cheerful, the menu a sprightly trawl of ideas and ingredients from Europe and beyond. Fresh fish is a particular strength. A three-course lunch will cost around £15, a three-course à la carte evening meal around £25. There are lots of good New World wines on the wine list. Food is served daily, with the exception of Sunday lunchtime.

On the opposite side of the North York Moors at Wass, close by the picturesquely ruined Byland Abbey, you can find **The Wombwell Arms (tel. (01347) 868280)**,

Egon Ronay's UK Newcomer Pub of the Year 1992. Believed to occupy the site of the Abbey's granary, this low-beamed, stone-flagged inn dates back to the late 1600s. There are three dining rooms in which you can enjoy food from an eclectic bistro-style blackboard menu based around local fresh produce. Three courses will cost you £13 or so. Food is available every day except Mondays.

The Fauconberg Arms Hotel (tel. (01347) 868214) in nearby Coxwold is a good place to fortify yourself before or after a visit to Shandy Hall, home of eccentric 18th century novelist Laurence Sterne. The Fauconberg Arms is an unspoiled, family-run coaching inn which predates Sterne by a century or so. Here you can consume inventive, good quality home-made food in the dining room or one of two comfortable bars. Three courses will cost around £13, and meals are available seven days a week during the summer. The thoughtful wine-list pays particular attention to the New World.

Helmsley, a touch to the east, is a popular and attractive small town. **Monet's (tel. (01439) 770618)** at 19 Bridge Street is a sprightly three-storey building dating from the early years of the last century. Here the Dysons, a husband-and-wife duo of classical-French-trained chefs, provide a highly imaginative menu daily except Monday evenings. The surroundings are elegant, the service is friendly and the food is presented with exceptional care. Three courses à la carte will cost you £30 or so, or you can opt for the 'Surprise' menu which offers six mystery courses and five glasses of wine for £38. It is essential to book for the latter, and advisable to do so at other times.

A few steps away in the High Street, **The Feversham Arms (tel. (01439) 770766)** is a solid hostelry built in 1840 on the site of its predecessor. It offers traditional English cooking with a particular emphasis on fresh fish, shellfish and game. Meals can be taken in the small, friendly Goya restaurant, or you can choose from an extensive list of bar snacks. A three-course bar meal will add up to around £12, and the table d'hôte evening dinner costs £20 for three courses. There is certainly no shortage of wines to choose from, with around 240 bins listed. They include a number of interesting and unusual Spanish wines – try them while you have the opportunity!

A couple of miles south-east of Helmsley is the village Harome, in whose High Street stands **The Star (tel. (01439) 770397)**. It recently reopened last year, to be immediately hailed as Yorkshire Post Restaurant of the Year. Take a close look at the furniture in the bar – it comes from the workshop of 'Mousey' Thompson in nearby Kilburn. The food on offer is modern British cuisine with one or two interesting slants. Three courses will cost you around £17. The coffee loft upstairs is a pleasant place to take an after-dinner drink. Whilst the food is unquestionably excellent, some people have found the front-of-house style a little unbending. Judge for yourself.

Hovingham is a picturebook village on the B1257 between Helmsley and Norton. **The Worsley Arms (tel. (01653) 628234)** is a long, low, late-Georgian hostelry set on the village green, originally built to accommodate visitors to the spa. Today it houses an à la carte restaurant and a more informal – and slightly less

GOOD FOOD GUIDE ROUTIERS MERCIER CORP D'ELITE WINE AWARD SIGNPOST
AA 2 STAR & 2 ROSETTE RESTAURANT RAC 2 STAR RESTAURANT HOSPITALITY GOOD PUB OUTSTANDING FOOD AWARD
EGON RONAY JOHANSENS BEST LOVED HOTELS OF THE WORLD ASHLEY COURTENEY ROUTIERS
ALES
Liz & Ray Hopwood invite you to
discover the special atmosphere of the Drovers Bars,
The Silks Room & The Clubroom Restaurant
KINGS ARMS HOTEL
ASKRIGG IN WENSLEYDALE
NORTH YORKSHIRE DL8 3HQ
01969 650258 FAX 650635
Email rayliz@kahaskrigg. prestel. co. uk
YORKSHIRE LIFE 'HOTEL OF THE YEAR 1996' GOOD HOTEL CASSEROLE AWARD

expensive – bar and bistro. The menu is centred on hearty, traditional English food with a hint of French cuisine breaking through from time to time. A three-course dinner in the restaurant will cost around £25, or you can opt for the table d'hôte at £23.50 for four courses.

Kirkbymoorside was once an important staging post on the road between Thirsk and Scarborough. **The George and Dragon (tel. (01751) 431637)** at 17 Market Place is a charactersome old coaching inn whose huge fire is a real magnet in the colder months. As is evident from the décor, the landlord is something of a sports fanatic. The menu and the extensive selection of specials usually centre on locally-sourced game and fresh fish, but there are also interesting and innovative vegetarian dishes. Expect to pay around £17 for three courses. There is a good wine list – if you can resist the lure of the well-kept real ales.

Continuing eastwards to Pickering, it is worth taking the trouble to seek out **The Lodge Bistro and Hotel (tel. (01751) 472976)** in Middleton Road. Coming from Helmsley you will need to take a minor road left, off the A170, just before you reach the town itself. The Lodge is a Victorian gentleman's residence set in three acres of terraced gardens. The bistro is a conservatory, tastefully floored and furnished in stripped pine – and you can sit outside in favourable weather. Menus offer a good geographical spread of tastes and textures for those who are looking for something a little out-of-the-ordinary. A three-course à la carte dinner will cost you £19 or so. There is an ongoing programme of live music and special evening events. Closed Sundays.

The White Swan Hotel (tel. (01751) 472288), in Pickering Market Place, began life in the 16th century and has been added to steadily ever since. At the back of the property are signs of an aerial walkway which once linked this property with its neighbour, supposedly for the benefit of salt smugglers. The menu in the restaurant and bars is modern English. A three-course à la carte meal in the restaurant will cost around £16. Fixed-price lunches start at £7.95 for two courses, and are served seven days a week. The wine list specialises, rather unusually, in St Emilion Bordeaux.

Heading towards the coast, **Grinkle Park Hotel (tel. (01287) 640515)** lies on a quiet minor road between the A174 and the A171 near Easington. The winding approach to this grand, mock-Tudor country house is particularly spectacular when the rhododendrons are in flower. The restaurant is open seven days a week, and serves a mixture of French and Italian dishes – along with some delicious home-made sweets. There is a fixed-price three-course menu at £18, or you can choose three courses à la carte for approximately £25. Bar meals can be taken in a charming conservatory.

The Mallyan Spout Hotel (tel. (01947) 896206) at Goathland, in the heart of the Moors, is named after the 70ft waterfall which lies in the steep, rocky valley behind it. The hotel was purpose-built in the 1890s to cater for the visitors brought by the newly-opened railway. Today its menu offers modern English cooking with a variety of Continental and Eastern flavours. The restaurant has a fixed-price menu at £19.50 for three courses plus coffee. Alternatively you can

choose from a good spread of sophisticated bar snacks. The wine list runs to around 100 bins, with particular strength in New World and French wines.

It would be a sacrilege to visit Whitby without indulging in some of the seafood which lands daily on the Fish Quay. Two places stand head-and-shoulders above the rest, and a visit to the town can hardly be considered complete unless you have compared the two. **Trenchers (tel. (01947) 603212)** in New Quay Road just opposite the station is a busy modern-style diner which serves huge portions of fresh fish and shellfish – pretty much anything and everything available that day. A wide range of salads is also on offer, along with home-made vegetarian dishes. Three courses will cost you around £12. The atmosphere is lively, and the service is cheerful. Open 11am-9pm daily from Easter to the end of October.

In terms of price, quality and popularity **The Magpie Cafe (tel. (01947) 602058)** on Pier Road is directly comparable: both venues offer good value, ample Yorkshire cooking, and both generate huge queues at peak times. The Magpie is set on two floors, overlooking the harbour, in a quirky house that once belonged to the Scoresby whaling family. At least a dozen varieties of seafood will be on the menu each day, along with salads, vegetarian options and around thirty home-made desserts. Like Trenchers, it features prominently in the food guides and listings – and rightly so. Open 11.30am-9pm seven days a week from Easter until the end of October.

For a rather grander albeit hugely pretentious experience in Whitby, try **Larpool Hall (tel. (01947) 602737)** in Larpool Drive on the southern outskirts of the town. Larpool Hall is a Georgian country house, with décor in character, which stands just across the Esk from the village of Ruswarp. Its French-trained chef offers unusual and innovative combinations, presented with skill and attention to detail. The carte du jour at £20 gives you three courses, aperitifs and coffee, or you can choose a three-course evening meal à la carte for somewhere in the region of £22. There is a varied wine list, with some interesting and adventurous choices, including a Lebanese wine. Sunday lunch is not available, otherwise Larpool Hall serves food to non-residents seven days a week.

Last, but by no means least, is **East Ayton Lodge (tel. (01723) 864227)**, a mid-Victorian shooting lodge standing in its own extensive grounds at East Ayton, three miles south-west of Scarborough on the A170. It has three dining rooms, decorated in character with the building itself, where you can enjoy a varied English-Continental menu. There is a fixed price four-course menu at £22.50, or you can choose three courses à la carte for about £18. The wine list runs to 70 or so items, selected from around the globe. Standards of presentation and service are commendably high. Open seven days a week.

Sponsored by Carlsberg-Tetley

Yorkshire Jewels

The countless books on North Yorkshire would fill a library the size of Rutland. Romantic novels, rustic tales and groaning shelves of histories and guides all attract visitors who throng the major tourist centres every season. But often poorly guided, steered by the glossy brochures and increasingly by the lure of popular television series, many of these newcomers enjoy little of the real North Yorkshire. Here is a selection of special places which you might otherwise easily overlook.

A Magic Garden: Hackfall

Spectacularly sited in a gorge of the river Ure, Hackfall is a maze of majestic trees, wild flowers and contorted paths, the Hansel and Gretel illusion completed by a fantastic collection of follies. Follow the labyrinth to the Rustic Temple, Mowbray Point, Fountain Pool, Weeping Rock, Forty Foot Fall, Fishers Hall and the Dropping Well... and do not lose your way! Will you find the golden beach?

The one hundred acres 'green garden', once described as 'one of the most complete birds-eye landscapes in the world' was laid out by William Aislabie around 1750 as a direct contrast to the more regimented scheme executed by his father at nearby Studley Royal. Inspired by an Alpine journey and funded from profits arising from investments in the South Sea Bubble, Hackfall became a regional attraction and for over 200 years was one of the most visited places in the North of England. Its recent decline culminated in threats from commercial forestry. Happily, destruction has been averted by the creation of the Hackfall Trust, the Woodland Trust and the Landmark Trust have taken over responsibility for the protection of the trees and a number of the follies.

Footpath access is opposite Hackfall Farm in the village of Grewelthorpe near Masham. An alternative footpath enters the woodland north of the village off the Masham road.

A Quintessential English Village: Nun Monkton

The Englishman languishing in the corner of some foreign field has a dream of home, a dream that is the reality of Nun Monkton. Rejoicing in the absence of a through road and embraced on two sides by the conjoining rivers Ouse and Nidd, this sleepy village has the serenity of a dozing swan.

Old cottages surround an expansive green graced by trees, a maypole and a duckpond, a leafy drive leading to a church, half - hidden by a magnificent weeping beech. The imposing 12th century St Mary's was formerly a chapel for nuns. An architectural gem it shares the riverbank with the handsome red-bricked hall built around 1690 in the Queen Anne style. In the grounds of the hall are a number of interesting 17th century statues. Beyond the garden wall, where the two rivers meet, is a languid expanse of water.

Overlooking the village green is the famous Alice Hawthorn Inn named after a legend of the turf. From seventy one starts in the 1840's this terrific animal notched up fifty-one straight wins.

Nun Monkton is north of the A 59, midway between York and Harrogate.

A Deserted Medieval Village: Wharram Percy

Wharram Percy is the site of a lost civilisation in the heart of the Yorkshire Wolds. A former agricultural community of several hundred souls, it suffered neither levelling at the hands of invaders, nor a natural catastrophe, the strange abandonment of the entire village arising, it is generally assumed, from economic decline and the diminishing price of wool.

The best known of some 40 such settlements in this part of Yorkshire, Wharram Percy has been extensively excavated in recent years, exhibits and displays in Malton Museum charting its 11th century history.

On rising ground, above the route of an abandoned railway track which affords picturesque access, are the sites of the village houses and the solitary ruin of the church of St Martin's. Some fragments of this date from the 10th century. In the shadow of its roofless nave is a delectable spring-fed pond, the most wonderful place for a picnic.

Wharram Percy is south-east of Malton, off the B1248.

A Holy Crypt: Lastingham

The power of this subterranean shrine to Saint Cedd is astonishing. For Christians and atheists alike, its aura knocks the spiritual Geiger counter off the scale.

Built in the 11th century by monks to honour the founder of Lastingham's monastery, it has remained largely untouched in over 900 years. Having an apsed end, it is thought to be unique in England.

Entered down a flight of stairs leading from the nave of St Mary's church, the crypt has a chancel, nave and side aisles and four massive Norman columns supporting the vaulted roof. These features are impressive enough but, illuminated by candlelight, the simple monolithic altar which bathes the senses is all you see.

In and around the church are many carved stones – crossheads, door jambs and shafts of great antiquity. The village of Lastingham also preserves two holy wells, and, above the door of the old post office, an inscribed maxim for contented living:

THE HAP OF A LIFE
GOOD OR ILL
THE CHOYCE OF A WIFE

Next to the church is the Blacksmith's Arms whose fine interior includes a preserved Yorkshire range and period furniture. This characterful inn was once kept by a hard pressed curate's wife who had 13 children.

Lastingham is north of the A170 between Helmsley and Pickering. Access is through Hutton-le-Hole or Cropton.

A Flowered Beck: Scalby Mills

The prettiest place in the whole of Scarborough gets fourteen visitors a year although this figure includes fishermen and may be exaggerated. It lies, paradoxically, not 200 yards from the captive tanks of the Sea Life Centre, its beck and bank sides supporting a host of wildlife including salmon, sea trout and brown trout, deer, heron, kingfisher and myriad flowers.

The Scalby Beck was joined, by an artificial cut, to the Derwent to prevent the flooding of that river in its lower reaches, the augmented flows debouching into Scarborough's North Bay. From its outfall, the beck can be followed along a short and sinuous but joyous course to the road bridge, passing glides, cascades, tiny islands and one substantial waterfall. Part of the route which, as a result of landslip, is uneven, passes through dense woodland filled with songbirds.

Within sight of Scarborough Castle and the throng of tourists, the unmolested Scalby Beck is the perfect place for quiet relaxation. Take a book, a sketching pad and a generously filled hamper and be unwound by the gurgle of the stream. Will you be the fifteenth visitor this year?

The Scalby Beck flows into the sea near the Scalby Mills Hotel. Just above the hotel on the bend of the steep road is a track. It leads over the hill to the beck side.

A Roman Town: Aldborough

A tile stamped LEG. IX HISPANA shouts a reveille that spans the centuries. 'The Ninth Legion Rule OK!' would be the equivalent call today. The famous ninth, who served with outstanding distinction in Spain and were chosen as one of four crack legions for the Claudian invasion of Britain,were stationed here, in what became known as Isurium Brigantum. From the first century they built an impressive military camp covering 55 acres. The camp and the developing town were protected by ramparts and by a wall of red sandstone, some of its foundations surviving today.

Within the boundaries of the now pleasantly landscaped old town,visitors can trace the lines of the walls, forum and grid of streets. On the site is a museum packed with exhibits such as coins, pottery and bronze objects, a back-scratcher, ear picks, nail cleaners and spatulae, although the real joy of Isurium is in its mosaic pavements. Two outstanding examples remain, one having been discovered in 1832 by a man who was burying a dead calf. Incomplete, it is thought to show a lion sitting under a tree. The second pavement, which is in near-perfect condition, has an eight-point star design surrounded by four decorative borders.

The Roman town is in the delightful village of Aldborough whose other treasures are a 15th century cross, a Georgian manor house, a maypole and the church of St. Andrew.

Aldborough is near Boroughbridge and is easily accessed off the A1.

Courtesy of Yorkshire & Humberside Tourist Board

A Miniature Minster and a Carnivores Cave: Kirkdale

The beautiful minster church of St. Gregory sits coyly beside the Hodge Beck, surrounding woodland guarding this gem of the dell. An Anglo Saxon church, it has a memorable interior and, above the south doorway, a unique Saxon sundial. Some seven feet long and two in width, it reads in translation : 'Orm Gamalson bought S. Gregorius' minster when it was all to-broken and to-fallen, and he let make new from the ground, to Christ and St. Gregorius, in Eadward's days the king, and Tosti's days the earl. This is the day's sun mark. And Hawarth wrought me, and brand the priest.'

The minster and its yew-shadowed churchyard are places for quiet contemplation, but there are other attractions close by. The attendant Hodge Beck, which seems strangely depleted of water even during wet weather, plays geological hide and seek, percolating through the porous limestone, a mile or so upstream. A ramble along its pooled bed can be quite rewarding, the keen eye discovering a host of fos-

sils. Near the footbridge, in the cliff on the eastern side of the beck is another curiosity, a cave, one of the first such ossiferous caverns ever explored in England. Bring your oldest clothes, boots and a torch and follow the example of Dr Buckland, who in 1821 explored this glacial den. Some 250 feet long with a height varying from two to fourteen feet, the cave was the home of savage creatures, Dr Buckland discovering a vast charnel house of bones belonging to tiger, bear, wolf, lion, elephant, rhinoceros, hippopotamus, horse, ox, deer.

Kirkdale is near Kirkbymoorside and the A170 Helmsley to Pickering road.

An Enchanted Lake: Gormire

The second largest tarn in Yorkshire, the enigmatic and brooding Gormire lies at the foot of the stupendous Whitestone Cliff and White Mare Crag. In olden times, the lake was said to be unfathomable and it still retains about its leafy banks an air of mystery. In a cup-like hollow the lake is about a mile in extent and is the source of numerous legends. Like Semerwater in Wensleydale, it is credited with hiding a beautiful city, another story prophesying that whenever the surface becomes covered with hay, the White Mare of Whitestone (another legend, associated with a plunge over the precipice by a horse) will carry it off on its back! One well believed local tale is that a goose sank beneath the waves and reappeared some days later featherless, alive and not quite oven ready, twelve miles away in Kirkbymoorside! Outlandish stories and recent talk of ghostly happenings apart, the lake is a real jewel and is well worth exploring. On its banks grow various species of wild flowers and the bog bean flourishes on the margins. This plant was used by Foggitt's, the botanical chemists in Thirsk. Bill Foggitt, the well known Yorkshire weather sage, remembers his father gathering herbs on the lake side.

Lake Gormire is east of Thirsk, off the A 170, near the infamous Sutton Bank.

The Final Resting Place of Oliver Cromwell (or at least part of him!) Newburgh Priory.

Begun in 1145, Newburgh Priory, which is open to the public, is still the home of the Earls of Fauconberg, and contains many family portraits, elegant furniture and a particularly fine water garden. Its most famous inhabitant is long since dead. The headless body of Oliver Cromwell is said to be secreted in a room on an upper floor. The headless corpse was brought to Newburgh by Mary, the Lord Protector's daughter who married into the Fauconberg dynasty. In 339 years, the cadaver has remained unmolested despite the determined attempts at discovery by another leader of England. A guest in the house, Winston Churchill, was disturbed in his attempts at uncovering the body and was soundly reprimanded.

Newburgh Priory is one mile south of Coxwold, which is off the A170 between Thirsk and Helmsley

A Moated and Crenellated House: Markenfield Hall

Seldom mentioned in any guide book, the finely preserved, privately owned Markenfield Hall stands all alone in farmland near Ripon, its reclusive character accentuated by fortified walls and a moat. An aloof but immensely interesting fortified manor house built by John De Markenfield in 1310, it is only open for inspection on Mondays from April until October.

Surrounded by farm buildings, Markenfield, which was once protected by a drawbridge, has a large dining hall, a kitchen with vaulted cellars, a chapel reached by a stair-turret, a neo-Tudor gatehouse and two 17th century lodges. Remarkably, it is the only fortified manor in Yorkshire to survive six hundred years intact, even the Scottish incursions, which left neighbouring Knaresborough in flames after the Battle of Bannockburn, leaving Markenfield unscathed.

Described as one of the most romantic houses in England, Markenfield has witnessed a succession of departing warriors, members of the illustrious family that lived here for centuries fighting at Agincourt and Flodden Field.

In 1569, the last of the lineage became involved in the ill fated Rising of the North. To escape capture and certain execution, Sir Thomas Markenfield fled to Flanders and his home was confiscated to the crown.

Markenfield Hall is between Harrogate and Ripon and is west of the A61.

A Limestone Wilderness: Kingdale

It is rare anywhere on earth to find a 12,000 year old wilderness unchanged and unused for man's rapacious purposes. Go to Amazonia and you will find one such place. Go to Kingsdale in North Yorkshire and you will find another.

The cracked and fissured desert of limestone above Ingleton has remained inviolate since the last ice-age. Formed millions of years ago by marine sedimentation, the limestone has since been weathered by water and ice, forming typical individual slabs of rock called clints, separated by deep cracks known as grikes which create a micro-climate for highly localised plants.

Above the road, on the hillside opposite Ingleborough, there is in one contorted gully whose maelstrom of rock is awesome, leviathan boulders, razor sharp blocks, some with gargoyled faces and tons of loose scree presenting a petrified frenzy. At the top of the incline are two even bigger monoliths named the Cheese Press Stones. In their symmetry they are distinct from the turmoil below, gazing out like mountain sentries.

The best way to access this wilderness is on foot from Ingleton. Follow the River Twiss upstream (small entry fee payable) passing a series of spectacular waterfalls, for about 1.5 miles and go right across a bridge. Go left on a descending track at the Ingleton Waterfalls sign and cross a footbridge over the river. Go left for 50 yards on the road and turn right, following a public footpath sign uphill. Stout boots must be worn.

Ingleton is between Settle and Kirkby Lonsdale on the B6255.

An Eloquent Castle: Wensleydale

'I mark my name on this fragile pane and wonder at the fragility of life.' In scratching 'Marie R' with her diamond ring, Mary Queen of Scots could well have pondered her fate. Like her, the window glass in the impossibly romantic Castle Bolton has gone, but the room of the most famous prisoner in Yorkshire history remains.

Captured after the Battle of Langside in 1568, Mary was taken to Castle Bolton and held in the custody of Lord Scrope for six months. She escaped but was recaptured and finally executed at Fotheringay in 1587. Much as she left it, her bedchamber at Bolton is open to view.

With four broken towers and a gaunt and menacing aspect that dominates the entire dale, this classically-built example of English military architecture dates from the 14th century and the reign of Richard II. Still occupied, the castle has, in addition to the regal apartment, an impressive great hall, a chapel, a horse mill, and in the grounds, a pleasant garden and a vineyard.

Mary whiled away her captive hours by reading and learning English from her tutor Sir Francis Knollys. She addressed her first letter in her new language to him: 'Mester Knoleis, I heve sum neus from Scotland...' The queen ended her missive, 'thus, affter my commendations, I prey God heuu you in his kipin. Your assured gud frind, Marie R.' There is a postscript: 'Excus my iuel writin thes furst tym.'

Castle Bolton is west of Leyburn in Upper Wensleydale.

Switzerland in Miniature: How Stean

Alpenhorns and the distant sound of yodelling may be absent, but everything else about How Stean has the character of an alpine chasm. Created by the percolating and scouring action of the Stean Beck and described by that doyen of Yorkshire walkers, Alfred J Brown, as 'a brawler, mutinously wild and violent', the 80 feet deep How Stean Gorge is a steep-sided limestone ravine clothed with a luxuriant growth of trees and festooned with rare mosses, lichens and ferns. A network of narrow paths and three high bridges are ideal perches for the observation of trout, grayling, dippers, kingfishers and wagtails. Adventurous visitors, torch in hand, may enter Tom Taylor's Cave, whose interior has been likened to the belly of a whale.

Further downstream, the beck marries the Nidd, the waters going on to the lovely village of Ramsgill and Gouthwaite Reservoir. This broad expanse of water is the favourite resort of bird watchers. Many rare waterfowl grace its banks and golden eagle have been seen in the area. On the far bank of the reservoir is the abandoned line of the Nidderdale Light Railway. An engineering marvel, it was built to aid construction of the Angram and Scar House dams in the high dale. The scenic route of the old track can be followed on foot.

Courtesy of Mary Symes

How Stean is north of Pateley Bridge on a beautiful winding road that terminates in the hilltop village of Middlesmoor. From here a rough track leads to the dams, over moorland inhabited by golden plovers.

A Life in Solitary: Mount Grace

King Henry VIII perpetrated the greatest act of vandalism in the history of England, the consequences of his papal quarrel being felt in the abbey-rich county of Yorkshire like no other. His Dissolution of the Monasteries brought an abrupt end to life in scores of religious houses across the region, his wrath falling on the Carthusian priory of Mount Grace – Yorkshire's only representative of the order – with a particular poignancy.

Unlike other brethren, the Carthusian monks lived the life of hermits, each brother remaining alone in his cell and vowed to perpetual silence. The strict regimes of the Carthusians did not endear the order to novices and, as recruitment to the fold was rare, not many monasteries were established. Consequently, the loss of the few houses that were built, was strongly felt.

Mount Grace, founded in 1398, is doubly precious as the best preserved Carthusian monastery in England. In a picturesque setting under the wooded slopes of the Hambleton Hills it preserves a wealth of fascinating remains which give some insight into the strict existence of prayer and self-denial. The spaciousness of a restored cell – each monk was allotted what amounted to a little two storey house consisting of a living room, study, bedroom, lavatory and a back garden – showed that in 1398, there were a few compensations!

Visitors will enjoy the monk's fishpond and the award winning exhibition in the 17th century manor house.

Mount Grace is near Osmotherley on the edge of the North York Moors National Park. Access is from the A19.

A Druids' Circle: Ilton

Come here at the time of the summer solstice and enjoy a mystical experience... without the riot police. A miniature Stonehenge, the druids circle at Ilton was erected on the instructions of William Danby, the owner of nearby Swinton Park. An early form of job creation, it gave work to unemployed men who were paid one shilling a day for the task of hauling and erecting the giant stones.

Set in dense woodland off a bumpy track nearly 3 miles south-west of Swinton Park, the circle is somewhat difficult to find,but its discovery only adds to the sense of mystery. To children brought up on the Tales of Narnia, it is doubly exciting.

The circle is the source of an amusing tale. Free food and an annuity were promised to any would-be hermit should he live in the stony precincts without speaking for 7 years. One tight -lipped recruit lasted nearly 5 years!

Ilton is south west of Masham overlooking Masham Moor.

A Secret Force: Near Askrigg

Waterfalls, fosses and forces. We have a number of names in Yorkshire for tumbling water, that magical ingredient in summer picnics, romantic paintings and films. Cascades like those at Aysgarth, the location for the stirring quarter-staff altercation in *Robin Hood – Prince of Thieves*, are internationally famous, although the inevitable crowds may detract from the experience. However, if you prefer a more private and intimate communion with nature, come to the twin forces of Mill Gill and Whitfield Gill.

Photogenic Aysgarth is all measured rush and gurgle. The dynamic duo in comparison have all the impetuosity of sky divers, leaping their ravines and hurtling downwards to the thunderous applause of the rocks fifty feet below. Around the spray soaked margins grow rare ferns and flowers, the torrents being the perfect habitat for that most Yorkshire of birds, the dipper.

The twin forces are near Askrigg in Wensleydale. Go west from the village past St Oswald's church, following a footpath marked 'Mill Gill Force'.

A Restored Walled Garden: Beningbrough

Walled gardens embowered and victualled some of the grandest homes in England but many have gone to dust. Joyously, this is not the case at Beningbrough Hall, where an ongoing five year project by the National Trust is restoring seven acres to delight the palate and beguile the senses.

Beningbrough's Victorian glory days

are blossoming once more, a 19th century variety of pea vying for attention alongside fifteen kinds of rhubarb, forty different types of apple and pear trees and a host of flowers and sweet-smelling herbs. The restoration work is providing new paths, cold frames, glasshouses, arches and beds and a rebuilt wall using reclaimed bricks. One star of an increasingly spectacular show is Lady Downe's Seedling, a richly flavoured white grape dedicated to a former lady of the house and originally raised by head gardener Thomas Foster in 1835. After enjoying the garden, visitors may sample its toothsome produce in the restaurant.

The elegant hall in a sylvan position overlooking the river Ouse was built in 1716. A repository for over a hundred paintings on loan from the National Portrait Gallery, it also accommodates a working Victorian laundry.

Beningbrough Hall is north-west of York and is signposted from the A19.

An Underground Labyrinth and an Abundance of Follies: The Forbidden Corner

The fantastical Forbidden Corner is part ghost train and part maze, a uniquely eccentric folly that distills the mythology of a thousand years in an eye-popping journey down subterranean passages, blind alleys and crepuscular trenches set in a 4 acre magical garden. At every turn you expect to meet Medusa or the Gorgon... and you do!

Through creaking doors and past peering faces and grottoes sprouting diabolical beasts, this is a fun-filled journey spiced with just a smidgen of fear, a sensuous appreciation of Alice In Wonderland and the Odyssey rolled into one.

Wharram Percy - Wolds

Children and adults alike will enjoy the unforgettable experience.

The Forbidden Corner was created as a private fantasy but it is now open to the general public on Sundays and Bank Holidays, Easter to October and on Saturdays in July and August.

The Forbidden Corner is located in Tupgill Park south-west of Leyburn and Middleham. Take the Coverdale Road over the moor, pass Coverham church and turn right into the park through the big iron gates.

Sponsored by Snowdens the Jewellers

In Full Bloom

North Yorkshire is fortunate in enjoying some of the finest gardens in the kingdom. Those described below range from vast acreages of formal plantings to cottage-style gardens. Whether you are looking for new ideas for your own patch, or simply for a chance to enjoy the results of someone else's labour, you are bound to find plenty to interest you here.

© Lynne Brotchie/G.P.L.

Duncombe Park, Helmsley (01439 770213/771115)

This early 18th century green garden takes up 35 acres in 300 acres of dramatic parkland and was described by Sacheverell Sitwell as "the supreme masterpiece of the art of the landscape gardener". According to the Guinness Book of Records, Duncombe Park also boasts the tallest ash and lime trees in the country, as well as some enormous specimens of beech, oak and ash – mostly dating from the original eighteenth-century planting. There are spectacular views of the North York Moors from the terrace.

Off A170 east of Thirsk, 1 mile south west of Helmsley. Open May to September, daily, 11am - 6pm. Entrance (garden and park): £2.95, children £1.50.

Shandy Hall, Coxwold, North of York (01347 868465).

Author Laurence Sterne wrote Tristram Shandy during the 1760s in the pretty 15th century cottage, Shandy Hall. The garden is full of season-long interest and has featured in the Good Garden Guide, Country Life and Period Living.

The plantings are in three sections. The Stackyard Garden has borders of herbaceous plants and shrub roses with views onto the North York Moors. The Old Garden is approached through a small orchard with trees covered with climbing roses. The third section is a sunken garden created in an abandoned quarry.

From York take A19, 7 miles from either Easingwold or Thirsk, turn east, signposted to Coxwold. Garden open May to September daily (except Saturday), 11am - 4.30pm. Entrance: £1.50.

Old Sleningford Hall, Mickley, near Ripon (01765 635229)

The present garden was established in the early 19th century and is a perfect example of its era. Owned by The Rt Hon and Mrs James Ramsden, this unusual three acre garden has extensive lawns, woodland and a beautiful lake with islands. The kitchen garden has a small watermill and the whole is bordered by yew and huge beech hedges. There is also a Victorian fernery. Home-made teas are available and plants are for sale on Open Days.

Five miles west of Ripon off B6108. After North Stainley take first or second left and follow signs to Mickley for 1 mile. Open on specific days, but owners are happy to receive visitors by appointment. Entrance: £2, children 50p.

Nawton Tower Garden, Nawton, near Helmsley (01439 771218)

Owned by the Douglas Ward Trust, this atmospheric 12 acre garden was created by the Earl of Feversham in the 1930s and includes several smaller 18th century compartmented gardens with a selection of rhododendrons, heathers, azaleas and old shrub roses. Every junction from the central walk leads to a fresh surprise: a yew-hedged topiary garden, a clearing with a stone fountain and a statue on a gazebo.

Take A170 from Helmsley towards Scarborough, and in Nawton and Beadlam village, turn left up Highfield Lane. After 2 miles entrance is through white gates. Open May and June, 2-6 pm, weekends only, and at other times by appointment. Entrance: £1.50, children 75p.

Constable Burton Hall, Leyburn (01677 450428)

The Hall, built in 1768 for Marmaduke Wyvill, is a perfect Georgian Palladian mansion designed by John Carr of York. Design began on this large romantic garden in 1932, and it has nature trails with a terraced woodland walk which drops down to a lake with lilies, roses, wild flowers and ferns. There is a fine selection of ancient trees including mature cedars shading the lawn, cherries, acers, maples, beech, oak and two grand avenues of lime.

On A684, three miles east of Leyburn, 6 miles west of A1. Open daily from March 22 to October 19, 9am-6pm. Entrance: £2, children 50p.

Harlsey Hall, East Harlsey, Northallerton

Owned by Sir Joseph and Lady Barnard, the garden consists of six acres of woodland and wonderful terraced lawns. In May the woodland is blanketed by bluebells. Other sites to note are the 18th Century Italian temple in the grounds and the traditional church on Saxon foundations. Home-made teas are available to visitors on open days.

Seven miles from Northallerton on the A684, Teesside Road. Turn left to east Harlsey, before Ellerbeck. At the Cat and Bagpipes Inn turn right. Open three times in the year, from 2-6pm. Entrance: £2.50, children £1.

Burnby Hall Gardens, Pocklington (01759 302068)

These wonderful gardens, close to York, have the finest display of hardy water lilies in Europe, forming part of the National Collection. The lilies may be seen from June to mid-September in a normal year, and in July the two lakes are covered in 80 different varieties of colourful blooms. The lakes are also home to a variety of interesting fish, both coarse and ornamental.

Off A1079, 13 miles east of York in Pocklington. Open daily 30 March to mid October (best season June to September), 10 am-6pm. Entrance: £2, children 50p.

Newby Hall, Ripon near Harrogate (01423 322583)

Covering 25 acres sloping down to the River Ure, the gardens at Newby Hall are designed to be at their best all year round. Their size allows for a great variety of rare and beautiful plants and trees including the National Collection of Cornus (Dogwood family). Also worth visiting are the White Garden, filled to bursting in the

Summer with white flowers, the Tropical Garden and the Orchard garden.
Close to the river is the stepped Water Garden filled by a gentle stream, and a walk lined with 19th century Venetian statues, Irish yew and purple plum. For children, there is an adventure garden and miniature railway. Lunches and teas are served in a licensed restaurant.
On B6265 four miles south east of Ripon, three miles west of A1. Open daily, except Monday, from Easter to September, 11am -5.30pm. Entrance: £4, children £2.70.

Parcevall Hall Gardens, Skyreholme near Skipton (01756 720311)
Well worth a visit for the glorious views of Wharfedale from the terrace and for the old rose garden, which has recently been renovated. For picnickers, there is an orchard with old varieties of apples. For the plantsperson, a fine range of rhododendrons, many originally collected in China, grow in the walk. Desfontainia, crinodendron and camellia abound.
Off B6265 Pateley Bridge/Skipton road, 1 mile north east of Appletreewick. Open daily, 28th March to 31st October (also in winter by appointment), 10am-6pm. Entrance: £2, children 50p.

Ling Beeches, Ling Lane, Scarcroft (01132 892450)
Featured on television and in The English Woman's Garden, this two-acre woodland garden was designed by the owner Mrs Arnold Rakusen with a view to labour-saving planting. Among the unusual trees and shrubs are some ericaceous plants, species roses, conifers, ferns and climbers.
From the A58 mid-way between Leeds and Wetherby, turn west at Scarcroft into Ling Lane, signposted to Wike at top of hill, garden one third of mile on right.

© Clive Boursnell/G.P.L.

Private visits are welcome by appointment only, telephone in advance.

Woodlands Cottage, Summerbridge (01423 780765)
An attractive enclosed cottage-style garden, formal herb garden and separate vegetable area form the main part of this one acre country garden. It has been developed over the past 10 years by owners, Mr and Mrs Stark, on a sloping site incorporating part of the existing woodland edge. There is a small nursery and teas are sold in aid of Muscular Dystrophy Society.
On the B6165 Ripley to Pateley road, half a mile west of Summerbridge. Open Sunday May 18 and August 10 (1.30-5pm) and for private visits by appointment. Entrance: £1.50, children 50p.

Tan Cottage, West Lane, Cononley (01535 632030)
Tan cottage, owned by Mr and Mrs Shaw, holds the national collection of primroses, as well as many old varieties of plants. The three quarter-acre garden adjoins the charming 17th century house.
Take A629 and turn off to Cononley just under three miles south of Skipton; at the top of the village turn right onto Skipton road. Private visits are welcome by appointment only, telephone in advance. Entrance: £1.50.

The White House, Husthwaite (01347 868688)
This one-acre garden is of particular interest to a plantsperson, as it was created from scratch in seven years and is now maturing. It contains a conservatory, herb garden, gardens within the garden and new landscaping and planting in the old orchard.
Turn right off A19, signposted Husthwaite, three miles north of Easingwold, and proceed one and a half miles to centre of village opposite parish church. Private visits welcome by appointment only, telephone in advance. Entrance: £2.

Fairview, Smelthouses, Summerbridge, Harrogate (01423 780291)
Although Fairview is a small garden comprising only a quarter of an acre, it is packed with unusual bulbs, alpines and woodland plants and holds three National Collections: hepatica, primula marginata and anemone nemorosa. The garden has recently been extended on a steep slope, on which is an alpine house, fernery, small nursery and large pond. Teas are available.
From B6165, 12 miles north west of Harrogate turn right in Wilsill Village to Smelthouses. Fairviews is immediately after the bridge on the right. Private visits welcome by appointment only, telephone in advance. Entrance: £1.50, children free.

Sheriff Hutton Park, Sheriff Hutton, (01347 878442)
A particular feature of the estate are the various walks which include the bluebell walk, the Lombardy poplar walk and a lakeside walk. Along the back of the house, originally a Jacobean hunting lodge, is a fine wisteria. To the East is a sunken rose garden, overlooked by a wide border of shrub and climbing roses. The original statuary and Ice House date from 1619.
Take A64 York to Scarborough road, turn left to Flaxton and Sheriff Hutton. Signposted on the approach to the village up what appears to be a private road. Open mid January to mid December except Bank Holidays, Monday-Friday, 10am-4pm. Entrance: £2.35, children £1.20.

Gilling Castle, Gilling East, York (01439 788238)
Outstanding scenery with terraces constructed on the south-facing side, four of which tumble down the slope from an expansive lawn at the top. A forest area and ornamental lakes are nearby and tours are given by boys from the prep school of which Gilling castle is part.
On B1363 York–Helmsley road, 20 miles north of York. Open July and August, daily, 10am–4pm. Entrance : £1.50, children free.

Aldby Parks, Buttercrambe (01759 371398)
A thoroughly romantic 15 acre garden restored in 1964 by the current owner Mr Winn with the help of a single gardener. The original terraced garden was by Thomas Knowlton in 1746, and the wooded hillside site includes the mound and dry moat of King Edwin and Queen Ethelburga's seventh-century castle. A grassy walk where kingcups, primulas and dark ferns grow along the river's edge reveals greylag geese and a selection of ducks.
Take A166 from York towards Bridlington, turn left at signpost to Buttercrambe and continue for half a mile past Gate Helmsley. Open 1st and 15th June, 2-5.30pm, private visits for parties welcome by appointment only, telephone in advance. Entrance: £2, children £1.

Secret Garden, 10 Sherwood Grove, Acomb near York (01904 796360)

Under an acre's worth of garden has been extended over 15 years to include rockeries, a pond and a fruit cage, but primarily extensive mixed plantings. Four greenhouses show vines, cactus, succulent and tender plant collections. A small nursery and teas are available.

Off A59 from York, turn left into Beckfield Lane opposite Manor School, a quarter mile before Western Ring road. Take first right, second left, garden hidden behind suburban semi. Open days 8th June and 27th July (10am -5pm). Private visits welcome by appointment only, telephone in advance. Entrance: £1, children free.

Harlow Carr Botanical Gardens, Crag Lane, Harrogate (01423 565418)

It is said that if a plant prospers here it will grow anywhere in the north, and Harlow Carr holds one of the best collections of moisture-loving plants as proof. It also hosts five National collections including hypericums, dryopteris and polypodium. The 68 acres have been developed over the past 50 years as a botanic garden (a "Wisley for the North") to include extensive woodland and streamside plantings, winter garden and wild flower meadows.

On B6162 Otley road, a mile and a half west of centre of Harrogate. Open all year, daily, 9.30am-6pm. Entrance: £3.40, children free.

Thorp Perrow Aboretum, Bedale (01677 425323)

Containing one of the finest collection of trees in the North of England, this aboretum holds over 2,000 species including the National Collections of ash, oak, walnut and lime. You can follow the tree trail and nature trail or wander at your will.

Signposted off B6268 Masham road, two miles south of Bedale. Open all year, daily, dawn - dusk. Entrance: £3, children £2.

© Gil Hanly/G.P.L.

Wytherstone House, Pockley (01439 770012)

Owned by Major and Lady Clarissa Collin, this large and expanding plantsman's garden has been created from a green-field site over the course of 25 years. As well as a newly created aboretum, there is a Mediterranean garden with 18 varieties of lavender, a spring garden with azaleas and rhododendrons, and magnificent views over the Vale of Pickering.

Take A170 from Helmsley towards Scarborough for two and a half miles then turn left at signpost for Pockley, past the church. Visitors welcome by appointment only, telephone in advance. Entrance: £2

Sutton Park, Sutton-in-the-Forest (01347 810249)

The parkland is said to have been moulded by 'Capability' Brown, and was planted by one of England's most distinguished garden designers, Percy Cane. The present owner, Sir Reginald Sheffield,

DUNCOMBE PARK

Stately Home &
National Nature Reserve
A Perfect Venue for a day in the Country!

Lord and Lady Feversham invite you to join them in exploring and experiencing the delights of Duncombe Park; the Mansion is set within sweeping terraces and temples and stands above the Rye valley. It offers dramatic views over the Nature Reserve and surrounding countryside. View the Mansion's restored principal rooms, typical of a late 19th century grand interior. End a perfect day with a visit to our Yorkshire Tearoom and Parkland Shop.

Free Car Park. Disabled access.

House & Garden
Good Friday to 2 Nov: 11am - 5.30pm
Apr/Oct: Sat to Wed: May to Sept: Daily
Parkland Centre & Nature Reserve
(Open to non-visitors to the house)
28 March to 2 Nov: Daily: 10.30am - 5.30pm

For further information:
Please contact Sally at the Estate Office
Helmsley, York YO6 5EB
Tel: 01439 770213 Fax: 01439 771114

Harrogate
Autumn Flower Show

12th, 13th & 14th September 1997

Great Yorkshire Showground Harrogate

Our showcase event features a magnificent array of beautiful flowers, vegetables and top produce. Plants on show and for sale from Britain's finest nurseries. With over 400 trade exhibitors displaying plants, gardening tools and accessories, an extensive Craft fair, Fine Country Foods and the Yorkshire Pantry, there is plenty to see and buy!
With most of the show under cover, ample free on-site parking and free admission for children under 16, the show offers great value for all the family!

For further information contact:
The North of England Horticultural Society
Tel: 01423 561049 or Fax: 01423 536880
Charity No: 702017

has carefully expanded the planting, and there are several fine features on the terraces including ironwork gazebos and a woodland walk leading to a temple.

On B1363 eight miles north of York. Open 30 March-1 October, daily, 11am-5.30pm. Entrance: £1.50, children 50p

Mount Grace Priory, Staddlebridge, Northallerton (01609 883494)

In 1993 the garden of a monk's cell in the ruins of the Priory Guest House was laid out following the original design that was found during excavation work.

The one acre turn-of-the-century garden of step terraces has also been recreated with rock plants spilling over the edges. A nature trail at the front of the Priory follows the moated pond and Old Monastery fish pond with some interesting and unusual wild flowers. A family of stoats lives in this garden and were featured in a recent television documentary.

On A19, 12 miles north of Thirsk, seven miles north east of Northallerton. Open April-September, daily, 10am-6pm (October, 10am-4pm) Entrance: £2.40, children £1.20

Ripley Castle, Harrogate (01423 770152)

A striking feature of this garden is its recently restored formal areas. Nearby, the huge herbaceous borders are more than 120 yards long and amongst the most spectacular in the North of England. Also worth a visit are the magnificent 18th century orangery and summer houses.

The garden houses the National Collection of hyacinths which here are complemented by a rich variety of spring flowering bulbs. Visitors can also enjoy a lakeside walk through the deer park which gives fine views over the 'Capability' landscape below.

Off A61 Harrogate to Ripon road, three and a half miles north of Harrogate. Open April-October (daily) 11am-5pm; November to December 23rd 11am-3.30pm. Entrance £2.25, children £1.

Stillingfleet Lodge, Stillingfleet (01904 728506)

A plantsman's garden of about one acre subdivided into small gardens, each with a different colour scheme and emphasis on foliage plants and climbing roses and clematis. A wildflower meadow and natural pond are attached to the garden, together with a new 50 metre herbaceous border. The garden is home to the National Collection of pulmonarias.

From A19 York to Selby road take B1222 signposted Sherburn In Elmet. In Stillingfleet turn opposite the church; garden is at the end of the lane. Open May and June Wednesday 1-4pm and 1.30-5.30pm. Entrance £1.50, children free.

Sledmere House, Great Driffield (01377 236637)

Dating from the 1770s, Sledmere is one of the most well-preserved of 'Capability' Brown's landscape schemes. The characteristic belting and clumping of trees on carefully controlled diagonal vistas is spectacular. To the rear of the house is a newly planted knot garden and an Italian paved sculpture court dating from 1911. The 18th century walled garden is planted with mainly herbaceous plants and is entered through a small attractive rose garden.

Signposted off A166: nine miles north west of Great Driffield. Open daily (except Friday and Monday) Easter-September 11am-5pm. Entrance: £1.50, children £1.

Shore Things

Courtesy of Laurie Campbell

The North Yorkshire coast is undoubtedly one of the most varied and interesting stretches of seaboard in the country. Within the span of a mile or less, its character can shift from desolation to cosiness — and then back again. The 'coast' roads (the A174 and A171) generally stay well back from the sea, and points of access for vehicles tend to be relatively few and far between. Fortunately, there is a long-distance footpath, the **Cleveland Way**, which runs the whole length of the coast. It is, for the most part, both well-marked and well-maintained. However, regardless of whether you are on foot or in the car, you will find the Ordnance Survey's **Outdoor Leisure Map 27** (North York Moors East) a good investment. It covers all the places discussed here, at the generous scale of 1:25,000.

Not strictly in North Yorkshire, but just within the boundaries of the North York Moors National Park, is Boulby Cliff. At 666ft, it qualifies as the highest point on England's Eastern seaboard and the country's second highest coastal cliff. Don't expect a sheer rock face though, as the whole of this coast is constantly crumbling away into the North Sea, and Boulby Cliff has been still further undermined by two or three centuries of quarrying for alum. What remains is an imposing heap rather than a dramatic plunge. The view from the top is nevertheless breathtaking, especially in the teeth of a sea breeze. Boulby potash mine, to the south, is a dusty eyesore, but it does at least offer a present-day reminder of the mineral industries that once dominated the economy of the area. The easiest way to reach **Boulby Cliff** is to take the minor road to Boulby village, which leaves the A174 opposite the mine. Half a mile's walk north-west along the

Cleveland Way brings you to its peak.

The quirky fishing village of **Staithes**, less than two miles down the coast in the direction of Whitby, provides a complete change of mood. Parking in the old part of Staithes is tightly controlled, so use the car park in the newer part of the village, (which lies directly to the north of the A174) and walk down the steep hill to the harbour. At the bottom you will find an extraordinary jumble of tightly-pressed cottages, separated by narrow alleyways and flights of steps, jammed into the deep valley gouged out by Staithes Beck. Here, as in other small ports on this coast, you can usually see a few of the brightly-painted cobles — traditional flat-bottomed fishing-boats — still used by the local fishermen to set their lobster-pots.

From Staithes to **Port Mulgrave** is little more than a mile's easy walk south-east along the Cleveland Way. Only the latter half of this section of path actually runs along the cliff edge, but the views which greet you as you approach your destination are impressive. The alternative is to follow the A174 to Hinderwell and turn off at the north end of the village by St Hilda's church. The harbour at Port Mulgrave was built in the last century to ship iron ore to the industrial centres of northern England and was served by a mile-long underground tunnel. The harbour was rendered obsolete by subsequent construction of the coastal railway — itself now long-closed. With care, you can pick your way down the steep cliff and stand on the derelict jetty.

Runswick Bay is a mile or so off the main road, hence more easily missed than Staithes. There is a car park at the bottom of the precipitous hill which leads down to the village, but the spaces not occupied by locals are quickly snapped up at peak times, so the best policy is to park higher up, just past the pub on Runswick Bank Top. Runswick Bay is a little less charming than Staithes, and noticeably more commercialised, but whereas Staithes is firmly locked in between massive cliffs, Runswick Bay has the benefit of a generous and sheltered crescent of sandy beach running west towards Kettleness. Even on the busiest days, the western end of the bay, where the sand begins to give way to shelves of rock, can be eerily quiet.

All that remains of **Kettleness** is a handful of undistinguished cottages, a coastguard station and a pub perched on top of the cliffs. The main part of the village slid into the sea in 1829. As the presence of the coastguard station suggests, there are fine views to both east and west. This fact has been exploited for many centuries, as the grassy mounds at **Scratch Alley**, just south of Kettleness, attests. Beneath lie the remains of a Roman signal station, one of a series along this coast designed to give early warning of Norse invaders. Down near the shoreline it is possible to find a wide variety of fossils, and the bones of plesiosaurs and ichthyosaurs were discovered here in the last century. The cliffs, however, are still unstable and the tides rise sharply, so it is essential to be vigilant.

South from Kettleness is another excellent section of cliff-walk. If you prefer to drive, you will find the A174 plunging down the vertiginous **Lythe Bank** to run alongside the sea for a brief span at **Sandsend**. Extending from here to Whitby, you will find the best stretch of beach between Staithes and Scarborough: a good two-

and-a-half miles of increasingly sandy shoreline. For once there is adequate parking — directly on the sea front if you are lucky. The older houses in Sandsend are clustered on either side of the beck which scampers down from **Mulgrave Woods**. These woods belong to Mulgrave Castle, home of the Marquis of Normanby. The house itself is not open to the public, but pedestrians are allowed access to the woods on Wednesdays, Saturdays and Sundays (except in May). Deep within them, you can see ruins of the original Mulgrave Castle and, further back still, the site of Foss Castle, an 11th century motte-and-bailey castle.

At low tide it is very pleasant to stroll along the shore from Sandsend to Whitby, especially on a warm summer's evening. You can see your destination from the very outset, and it is mildly galling to find that after half-an-hour's stiff walking it doesn't seem significantly closer. One consolation is that even during the busiest periods you can usually find relative peace at **Upgang Beach**, the half-way mark. The soft shale along the strand is pierced, like a Swiss cheese, with centimetre-wide holes bored by bivalve molluscs known locally as 'piddocks'. Something about the run of the tides causes huge quantities of driftwood to be washed up here, along with the usual mounds of gaily-coloured plastic maritime debris.

Whitby is one of the most remarkable towns in Britain, despite the overwhelming tackiness of most of its supposed tourist attractions. Avoid visiting The Dracula Experience (unless obliged to by younger members of the party), but by all means read the earlier chapters of Bram Stoker's Dracula itself. The descriptions of the town are accurate and informative. In Chapter VI, for example, heroine Mina Murray reports of the view across the Esk from the Victorian quarter of **West Cliff** that "the houses of the old town are all red-roofed, and seem piled up one over the other anyhow, like the pictures we see of Nuremberg... Right over the town is the ruin of Whitby Abbey... a most noble ruin, of immense size, and full of beautiful and romantic bits... Between it and the town there is another church, the parish one... This is, to my mind, the nicest spot in Whitby, for it lies right over the town, and has a full view of the harbour and all up the bay to where the headland called Kettleness stretches out into the sea."

Whitby Abbey, now under the care of English Heritage, is open daily from March to October; call (01947) 603568 for details of times and prices. The parish church which Mina mentions, **St Mary's**, is ignored by many of the visitors who haul themselves up the 199 steps above Tate Hill Pier — a great shame, since it is quite unique. Inside you will find a multitude of 17th and 18th century box pews, ranked on two levels. They could seat, it is said, 2,000 individuals in the church's heyday. They are arranged around a massive three-decker pulpit dated 1778. Attached to it are two 'vamping horns', trumpet-like devices to allow the hard-of-hearing to enjoy the sermon. There are plenty of other fascinating features to enjoy, including Norman chancel windows and a Baroque brass chandelier.

At the foot of the cliff beneath St Mary's, **Henrietta Street** is gradually slipping into the sea. **Noble's** is in no imminent danger, which is fortunate, since it is a family business which produces some of the finest kippers in the country. A peek inside their tar-caked smokeroom is enough to make even the most hardened smokers concerned about the state of their lungs, but the kippers which emerge from it are succulent and melting — and stunningly good value.

Back across the **swing-bridge**, on the West side of the Esk, the **Fish Quay** is busy in the early hours of weekday mornings unloading and despatching the catch of Whitby's diminishing but dogged trawler fleet. By late morning the action here is largely over, and it is the amusement arcades at the foot of the Khyber Pass which are the source of noise and bustle. A walk to the end of **West Pier** offers fine views out to sea and back to the town. There is an even finer view from the top of the stone light-tower at the end of the older section of the pier, but it is open to the public only irregularly.

The access gangway to **East Pier** has been closed for some time, due to the landslip at the end of Henrietta Street. It is possible to slither across the rocks to it during low tide, but you are likely to find

Courtesy of Laurie Campbell

yourself alone bar a few sceptical seabirds and the occasional tight-lipped fisherman. Beyond East Pier in the direction of **Saltwick Nab** is prime fossil-hunting territory, a good place to chip an ammonite or belemnite from the crumbling shale. Take proper tools, or you will undoubtedly break your prospective trophy whilst extracting it. Only during the lowest tides of the year are you likely to find good specimens on the seaward rock shelves, as the most regularly-exposed areas will have been gone over pretty thoroughly by previous visitors. Constant erosion is always revealing new items of interest in the cliffs, but the crumbling rock is potentially dangerous. What is more, it is easy to get so absorbed in what you are doing that you are cut off by the rapidly-rising tide — so keep your wits about you.

A safer way to enjoy some spectacular fossils is to take a trip to **Whitby Museum** in Pannett Park. The Museum is a little way out of town on the west side of the Esk, and consequently receives far fewer visitors than it deserves. It is a wonderfully unspoiled museum, its ancient glass cabinets crammed with the most unlikely and bizarre curios. Here you can see, amongst other things, a narwhal's tusk, a ship's biscuit, a mummified hand carried as a charm by superstitious burglars and a 'Tempest Prognosticator' — an ingenious attempt to forecast the weather by monitoring the behaviour of leeches. More conventional exhibits include relics of the whaling industry, a huge amount of Whitby jet jewellery and a collection of items relating to Captain Cook and his expeditions. And, of course, there are the fossils, including an ichthyosaur and some massive molluscs. It all makes the gaudier attractions in the town centre seem positively dull. The museum is open daily; call (01947) 602908 to confirm times.

In Chapter VIII of *Dracula,* Mina Murray and Lucy Westenra walk along the clifftops to **Robin Hood's Bay**, where they enjoy "a capital tea... in a sweet little old-fashioned inn, with a bow-window right over the seaweed-covered rocks of the strand" before making the return journey. Their hike is no small undertaking, being a round trip of some 15 undulating and winding miles along the Cleveland Way. Less hardy souls can take the A171 from Whitby towards Scarborough and turn off left at High Hawsker. Once again it is a question of parking at the top of the cliff and walking down into the village, another ruthlessly picturesque fishing community which is nowadays capitalising on its reputation as a one-time haunt of smugglers. Its attractions include a folk museum, numerous gift shops and cafes, and a rather good second-hand bookshop.

Ravenscar, at the far end of the bay, consists of a Nonconformist chapel, a scatter of odd houses and **Raven Hall**, a large and gloomy hotel dating from 1774. What intrigues the passer-by, though, are the overgrown roads which set off purposefully to nowhere in particular. The solution to the mystery is that roads and the handful of Victorian houses represent the remnants of a grandiose scheme planned by a group of speculators in the 1890s. Impressed by the phenomenal success of the resort of Scarborough, they hoped to make their fortunes by repeating the story here. One subtlety which they overlooked was the fact that the eroding and unstable cliffs make access to the sea extremely difficult, and the security of anything built on the clifftop somewhat dubious. Unsurprisingly, the project soon came to grief.

The rugged stretch of cliffs between Ravenscar and Scarborough is singularly devoid of settlements, and is not easy to reach by road. For a pleasant and fairly unchallenging circuit, park at Cloughton and take the lane which runs seaward from the sharp bend on the A171. This will lead you down to the secluded inlet of **Cloughton Wyke**. Heading north along the clifftops you will soon be rewarded with a marvellous view back towards Scarborough. Continuing north brings you to **Hayburn Wyke**, a tiny wooded bay with its own waterfall. Hayburn Wyke is now a nature reserve maintained by the Yorkshire Wildlife Trust, and the steep woods are noted for their wide range of birds, plants and insects. Head up the valley and you will find a useful information board. You will also find the secluded **Hayburn Wyke Hotel**, which offers the chance of morning coffee, lunch or afternoon tea. From here it is an easy matter to return to your starting point along the disused track of the Scarborough-Whitby railway or retrace your steps along the coast.

It is easy enough to see why **Scarborough** was the Victorians' favourite resort. The massive headland at whose base the town is clustered has a fine, sandy bay to either side. The two beaches taken together almost equal in their extent — and perhaps surpass in their quality — the stretch between Sandsend and Whitby. **Scarborough Castle**, which stands on the headland, is well worth a visit. There are striking views back up the coast towards Ravenscar and south towards Cayton Bay and Filey. The castle's three-storey keep once stood a floor higher, and its massively thick walls are still awe-inspiring. Closer to the cliff-edge are the foundations of another Roman signal station. Scarborough Castle is open daily from March to October; call (01723) 375463 for details of times and prices.

Scarborough's appeal today depends on its remarkable mixture of high-Victorian architecture and 20th century tackiness. All the raucous attractions which typify the British seaside resort are here, but the town still retains a certain dignity. Away from the modern precinct, with the usual selection of High-Street names, you can browse away an afternoon in street after street of quirky cafes, delicatessens, second-hand book dealers and junk shops.

The **Rotunda** on Vernon Road is a domed, circular tower built in 1828 for the Scarborough Philosophical Society to house its collection of geological exhibits. The two floors and the gallery are linked by spiral staircases, and the walls are lined with the original showcases. Today they display a variety of interesting exhibits relating to local history and archaeology. Beneath the dome runs a ring-shaped frieze demonstrating the geology of the Yorkshire coast. The Rotunda is

© Mike Kipling

open Tuesday to Sunday during the summer. Call (01723) 374839 for further information.

Scarborough's **Art Gallery**, in the elegant surroundings of **The Crescent** has six oils by the popular Victorian artist Atkinson Grimshaw — five of Scarborough and one of Whitby — alongside many other works of local interest. It is open daily, excepting Mondays, during summer; call (01723) 374753 for details. Next door is the **Wood End Museum of Natural History**. Once the home of the Sitwell family, the West Wing still contains their books and a variety of other effects. Open daily, bar Mondays; for more information call (01723) 367326.

Finally, a real gem of a building, and very much a product of the period when the town was at its heyday, is the church of **St Martin's on the Hill**, Albion Road. Built in the 1860s in the neo-Gothic style, it has a rather ominous appearance when seen from the outside. Inside, however, it is a feast of Pre-Raphaelite ornamentation. The pulpit has ten painted panels designed by Rossetti, Ford Madox Brown and William Morris. Morris was also involved in the decoration of the ceiling and other parts of the interior. There is a painting by Burne-Jones on the altar wall, and the west windows are his too. Four rose windows by Rossetti and Morris — two of which won prizes in the 1862 Exhibition — can be seen in the chancel.

The suburban splendour of the better parts of Scarborough seems a far cry indeed from the bleak environs of Boulby mine where we began our journey, but both are equally the result of the Industrial Revolution, an upheaval which has marked this coast in so many ways. Add to this the natural beauty of the shoreline, the rich geology and the quaint disorder of medieval fishing communities, and the result is an extraordinarily complex and revealing landscape. It takes time and effort to come to grips with all it has to offer, but that effort is sure to be amply repaid.

Sponsored by Scarborough Borough Council

BLACK SHEEP BREWERY VISITOR CENTRE
'Shepherded Tours'
Sheepy Shop
Video
Bistro
Baa...r
& Much more!!
Open 7 days a week
For groups or individuals contact:
Lisa or Helen

BLACK
SHEEP
BREWERY
Wellgarth, Masham, Ripon,
North Yorkshire HG4 4EN
Tel: (01765) 689227

Family Forays

In England's largest county, all roads lead to a grand day out. Wild moors and sleepy dales, seaside fun and bustling cities. Around each new corner there's always more to delight and surprise you.

Bordering the southern edge of the **North York Moors National Park,** Ryedale has more to offer than glorious scenery and picture-postcard villages. A good place to start, the 2.5 acre, open air **Ryedale Folk Museum (01751 417367)** provides a 'snapshot' of country life in times gone by through its fine collection of tools, implements and household appliances. Amongst the exhibits displayed in its 12 traditional buildings is the oldest photographic studio in the country.

The classical temples of **Rievaulx Terrace (01439 798340)** are perhaps the best vantage point to admire **Rievaulx Abbey (01439 798228)**. Built by the Cistercians, this is one of England's most outstanding abbey ruins, set magnificently in a narrow, cosy valley.

Its a quick march from here to **Eden Camp (01653 697777)**, near Malton, to tackle the assault course. Designed for army training purposes, it was used to house Second World War prisoners. You'll really feel part of the action in the 29 original huts where wartime scenes are brought to life with sound effects, lights and even smoke!

The military theme is continued across the Wolds at **Elvington** near York, where you'll discover the **Yorkshire Air Museum (01904 608595)**. Both an attraction and a memorial to the men who served here in the last war, the preserved huts are filled with World War II memorabilia, uniforms and equipment. Special displays pinpoint the invaluable contribution made to the war effort by the Air Gunners and by Sir Barnes Wallis, who developed the bouncing bomb. Delve deeper in the reference archive, or simply marvel at the famous planes on show. Among them are a Mosquito, a Messerschmitt ME109G and the only remaining complete example of a Handley Page Halifax Bomber.

The action is of a different kind at **Flamingo Land (01653 668287)**, where the family fun includes not only thrilling white-knuckle rides, laser shows, but the animal magic of a zoo. More sedate by far, ride from Pickering to Grosmont on the **North York Moors Railway (01751 472508)**. Just the ticket for a relaxing, nostalgic trip by steam train through 18 miles of unspoilt moorland – the setting for Yorkshire TV's *Heartbeat*. Travelling through Newtondale, alight at Levisham to combine your ride with a walk. **Newton upon Rawcliffe** might be stuck in a timewarp, so little have the passing decades altered it. The star turn here is the home-baked tea, complete with melt-in-the-mouth scones, at the **Secret Garden Tearoom and Post Office (01751 472502)**. Definitely worth the three-mile-round hike from the station.

The many secluded caves and inlets along the coast afford excellent shelter – and privacy for clandestine activities. In past centuries the whole area was a free-trader's delight. Pre-eminent among such rogues, was John Andrew, 'The Smuggler King'. His story is outlined at **The Saltburn Smugglers Heritage Centre (01287 625252)**. Within the walls of his pub, The Ship Inn, daring coups were planned and vast quantities of contraband changed hands. Even when he was caught red-handed, influential friends

helped to keep him out of jail. He ended his days a free and wealthy man, having spent only two years behind bars.

Scarborough, England's oldest holiday resort, fulfils everyone's ideal of a seaside destination. In addition to miles of sandy beaches, donkeys and myriad amusements, the seafront miniature railway will carry you swiftly from the superb **Kinderland (01723 354555)** soft play adventure park to **The Sea Life Centre (01723 376125)** at Scalby. One of the biggest fish in Scarborough's pool of attractions, this is the place to take an underwater safari and watch as trained staff introduce inquisitive rays, lobsters and other amazing inhabitants of our native waters.

Winged creatures are the stars of **The Honey Farm (01723 864001)**, where you'll tour the hives and discover the fascinating world of the hard-working honey bee. It is said that a lifetime isn't long enough to learn all their secrets, but just one taste will tell you how special their honey is!

In the north-western corner of Yorkshire, fertile wolds and windswept moors give way to the peaceful splendour of The Dales. But near to Ripon, their southern gateway, it is speed rather than beauty which will take your breath away. **Lightwater Valley (01765 635368)**, approaching its 20th successful year, combines all the excitement of a major theme park with top-brand factory shopping. The landscaped green acres of the Park conceal an electrifying selection of adrenaline-pumping rides and childrens' entertainments. The sensational Ultimate is the world's longest rollercoaster, and the views from its 100 foot summits are spectacular – but plunging at over 60mph into the forest, you'll scarcely have time for the scenery! New for '97, The Hawk is unique in Britain. Not for the nervous, this pulse-racing ride swoops upside down before diving – with you in its clutches.

Adjacent to the fun-park, stroll along the cobbled streets of purpose-built **Lightwater Village** to discover bargains galore. In its relaxed, olde-worlde ambience, you'll find just the thing to re-vamp your wardrobe, home or garden. While the grown-ups shop, the children can tumble safely in the soft-play area, meet the animals at Old Macdonald's Farm or feed the ever-hungry ducks. A superb delicatessen echoes the tempting fare at the two coffee shops, and in the evening you can eat at The Hungry Hen Carvery.

Travelling westward through lovely Upper Nidderdale, there's plenty of opportunity to work off the extra calories exploring two of Yorkshire's most famous natural attractions. The gigantic gritstone outcrops of **Brimham Rocks (01423 780688)**, weathered by their exposure to the elements, are gnarled into fantastic shapes with equally fanciful names. A wonderful place for hide-and-seek, trying to fit the correct name to each formation, 'Gorilla', 'Kissing Chair' and 'Dancing Bear' may require an active imagination, but the 'Idol', its huge mass balanced on a one foot pedestal, is instantly recognisable.

Two miles out of Ingleton on the B6255 Hawes road, **White Scar Caves (015242 41244)** offer a chance to experience geological wonders of a different kind. This complex of underground caverns includes Britain's longest show-cave, a formidable 900 metres long. The guided tour will introduce you to an exciting vari-

Come and Visit

Betton Farm Rural Centre

Nr. Scarborough

Childrens Animal Farm

World of the Honey Bee

Farm Shop

Tearoom

Pottery Studio and Craft Shops

Open Daily
10am-5pm

Facilities for Disabled and Ample Parking

A Great Farm Attraction for all the Family

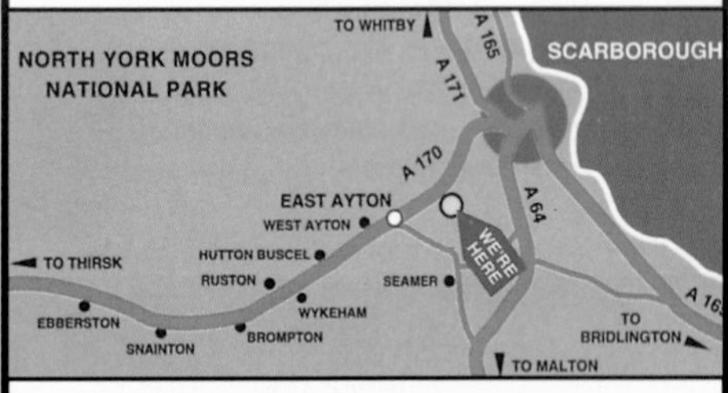

Betton Farm, Racecourse Road,
East Ayton, Scarborough,
North Yorkshire YO13 9HT
Tel: 01723 863143

ety of subterranean wonders, ranging from underground streams and waterfalls to the awesome Battlefield Cavern, carved out in the Ice Ages to a height of well over 100 feet. Safely back on the surface you can relax in the cafe, browse in the gift shop or enjoy the sunshine in the picnic area.

Stump Cross Caverns (01756 752780) at Greenhow, provide a further insight into the mysterious world beneath our feet. Half a million years ago, during their formation, bison, reindeer and wolverine took shelter among the intertwining passages and chambers. Sealed off during the last ice-age, the system remained undiscovered until the 19th century lead miners of this area accidentally broke through – revealing fabulous stalactites and stalagmites, animal remains and fossilised bones. Nowadays, skilfully lit steps and gravel paths lead through a wonderland of strangely shaped and coloured columns, curtains and pools to culminate in the Wolverine Cave – resplendent with magnificent formations.

A picturesque drive away across Appletreewick Moor, near Grassington, in the shadow of the 170 foot high Cow and Calf crags, **Kilnsey Park and Trout Farm (01756 752150)** uses the pure, crystal-clear, spring waters flowing from the limestone bedrock. Centuries ago, the monks of Kilnsey Grange channelled it into their stew-ponds. Today it yields delicious rainbow trout and attracts thousands to enjoy a host of water-based leisure activities. Watch the frenzy of the feeding area as trout scramble for your pellets, or use the traditional approach of rod, line and lure to catch a fresh and tasty dinner. Even children can have a go, with equipment, instruction and supervision all provided at the Fun Fishery. Non-anglers might prefer an adventure on horseback, trekking or trail-riding from the Kilnsey Trekking Centre, tackling the Adventure Playground, or simply browsing in the Plant Centre and Estate Shop.

There are more treats in store for committed shoppers at **Country Harvest,** Ingleton **(015242 42223)**, where, on a reclaimed two acre site, the farm shop concept has entered a new era. Inside the purpose-built barn you'll find a mind-boggling selection of fresh, local foods and specialities, together with country crafts, textiles, books and a bright, spacious coffee shop. Look no further for proper dry-cure bacon and air-dried ham; hand-made chocolates and scrumptious Penrith Fudge. A whole department is devoted to cheese in all its many guises. And to slake your thirst, why not sample Yorkshire Country Wines delicious, non-alcoholic, herbal Lakeland Punch.

En-route to Yorkshire's commercial heart, take a break at **The Darley Mill Centre,** Darley **(01423 780857)** for much more than a mill-shopping experience. Located in beautiful 17th century cornmill buildings, Darley Mill boasts one of the largest working waterwheels in the North. In addition to a full range of textiles and clothing, explore the miller's story, indulge in a full traditional lunch or light snack in the cosy restaurant or outside on the sunny terrace. The children will be in their element feeding the ducks or playing in the specially constructed play-area.

Far from being crumbling relics of Britain's manufacturing past, Leeds and Bradford are vibrant, prosperous and jam-packed

Run Wild!

The Hawk - New for '97! As launched by the Gladiators. The only ride of its kind the country. It will certainly ruffle your feathers!

The Ultimate Beast - The longest roller coaster in the world. Unleash yourself a tear through the wilds of the forest on this untamed beast.

The Sewer Rat - Scurry down into the sinister shadows on the country's only subterranean rollercoaster.

The Viper - Slither around the coil of this venomous adventure, it's a slippy specie

Falls of Terror - Plunge headlong into terrifying, raging rapids.

Many more rides for all the family!

For further information on opening dates and prices please call **01765 635368**

For excursion details contact your local coach company.

Lightwater Valley, North Stainley, Ripon, North Yorkshire HG4 3HT with a glittering array of first-class attractions.

Brand new for this year, the **Thackray Medical Museum (0113 2444343)**, which occupies the former Leeds Union Workhouse building, offers the perfect prescription for a fascinating day out. Appropriately enough, the £5 million venture is next door to St James's Hospital, but there the similarity ends. Inside, a collection of 23,000 medical objects trace the development of medicine through history and remind us of our 20th century good fortune.

Experience the streets of 1840, rife with disease, and learn how without anaesthetics or antibiotics a little girl's broken leg could cost her life. You'll see the horrors of the Victorian operating theatre, before leaping forward in time to the present for an introduction to keyhole, micro- and plastic surgery. Find out how our bodies work, and wearing an 'empathy belly', what it feels like to be pregnant.

Another recent addition, and a feather in the cap for Leeds, the prestigious **National and Royal Armouries (0990 106666)** collection of arms and armour opened last year. The new Leeds complex provides a permanent home for the National Collection and promises a thrilling, action-packed, interactive adventure for all.

At the heart of the new £42.5 million Leeds waterfront centre, you'll find five, themed galleries outlining the influence of arms and armour on the development of mankind through three millennia. The glories and horrors of war, the chivalry and spectacle of the Tournament, the splendour of the oriental civilisations and the history of self-defence are brought into sharp focus by live reports from the working television newsroom from areas of conflict world-wide.

Featuring the latest touch-screen computers, costumed re-enactments and 42 specially-made short films, you won't be lost for things to do inside. But step outside, and the exhibits really shine. Cheer on your favourite knight, jousting on horseback in the Tilt Yard. Watch the pageantry of military drill and mounted combat through the ages or marvel at hawks, trained to take another bird on the wing. Learn too how hunters track game using traditional breeds of dog, before visiting the animals' quarters in Menagerie Court. In the nearby Craft Court, you'll be fascinated to see the intricate, age-old crafts of the armourer, gun-maker and leather worker.

Close to the Royal Armouries, on Leeds' redeveloped waterfront, embark on an unforgettable adventure tracing the history of that Great British institution, the pub. At **Tetley's Brewery Wharf (0113 2420666)** you launch into a unique jaunt through the centuries as period room sets, conversation, sights, sounds and smells are introduced by a series of charismatic characters, beginning with the 14th century brewing monks.

Another popular attraction at the Brewery Wharf is the chance to see those gentle giants, the famous Tetley Shires, relaxing in their stables or demonstrating their working skill. There's always something happening at the amphitheatre or in the working crafts area, and, while adults tour the adjacent brewery, children can play to their hearts' content in the soft-play area or spacious playground.

Enter the lush environs of **Tropical World (0113 2661850)**, adjacent to

Canal Gardens and wander among banana, coffee and pineapple trees where 30 species of exotic butterfly flutter. In pools close to a tumbling waterfall you'll discover carp and terrapins, but thankfully the tree frogs and spiders remain safely screened. Recent additions include a fascinating desert environment, orchid house and, bathed in twilight, the nocturnal world of fruit bats, skunks and enchanting bush babies.

Motoring the short distance from Leeds to Bradford, head for the city centre Tourist Information Office – an annexe of the vast 'Pictureville' building which is home to the **National Museum of Film and Television (01274 727488)**. Not just a photographer's paradise, it's a must for anyone interested in the visual media. Encompassing everything from 'happy snapping' to video work, the galleries enable you to go behind the scenes in a TV studio, or catch up with your favourite programmes in 'TV Heaven' – the only archive of TV programmes and commercials in the country. While you're here, take in a performance at the only IMAX screen in the UK. The enormous 52 x 64 foot screen envelops you as you clutch your seat riding the rapids, or spinning through outer space.

Returning to earth, take the bus link from Bradford city centre, or motor round the ring road to find another new attraction, **Transperience Transport Discovery Park (01274 690909)**, close to the M62 junction 26. Just the ticket for a fascinating day out, jump aboard the tram, bus or trolleybus and explore the past, present and future of public transport at the Park's five centres. You can see for yourself the giant leaps in technology which have mobilised and motorised society, and explore forms of motive power other than the environmentally unfriendly car. On the mezzanine floor overlooking the energy gallery is the 'Maglev' train simulator, where, transported through time and space, you'll see dreams become a reality in 'The Future in the Past'. Next, the efficient 'Translink' service will deliver you to The Auditorium for a lighter look at the role transport plays on film and TV.

All change, to ride down to the workshop and view important restoration and maintenance work in progress, before you reach the end of the tramway and The Exploratory. Green signals go for all those who want to drive a train, change the bus route or grapple with the unseen objects hiding in the 'feelie-boxes'. You'll have trouble tearing the children away, so why not retire to the bright, spacious Terrace Cafe while they let off steam downstairs or in the safe, imaginative adventure playground.

As its name suggests, **Eureka! (01422 330069)** is about discovery. An instant hit with adults and youngsters alike, this Halifax attraction helps you really get to grips with science and technology. Themed areas are filled with hands-on exhibits specially designed to demonstrate mysterious aspects of everyday life. Not only will you find out how a lavatory works, but see what happens inside your body, and a working TV studio. There's lots for the under-fives to discover among the wobbly bridges and ball-pools of the 'Jungle', while the hero of the museum, Archimedes, takes regular plunges throughout the day. A truly captivating outing, your only problem will be persuading the family to leave!

Picture This

Courtesy of Mercer Art Gallery

North Yorkshire is rich in many things, but one of the area's better kept secrets is the number and quality of the numerous small art galleries tucked away in market towns and villages. Just as the landscape offers everything from steep wooded cloughs to limestone crags, heather-clad moors and stunning sea shores, so the galleries range from local framers offering inexpensive prints as a sideline to nationally-respected exhibition venues which attract a following from way beyond the county borders.

The distinctive limestone country of the western edge of the region that stretches north of Skipton up through Ingleton and over to the head of Wensleydale has to be high on everyone's list of favourite landscapes. It provides the backdrop to the **Linton Court Gallery (01729 822695)** in Settle. For more than a decade its exhibitions have featured young artists alongside nationally-respected painters, potters and printmakers. Next stop is Ingleton, with its houses nestling snugly in the steep valley under the brooding mass of Ingleborough. Here, during the summer months, the **Ingleborough Community Centre (01524 241701)** hosts exhibitions and offers courses on art and local and natural history, while just along the village street is the **Paul's Fold Gallery (01524 242375)** which has a comprehensive stock of watercolours of northern landscapes by a local artist. Once experienced, the thrilling views from the road from Ingleton over to Hawes will remain in the memory for ever, and so will the beautiful dale into which you finally descend.

Wensleydale, both dale and cheese, should never be rushed. Take it slowly and enjoy the string of pearls that lie along the valley of the Ure – historic towns and villages littered with ancient castles and

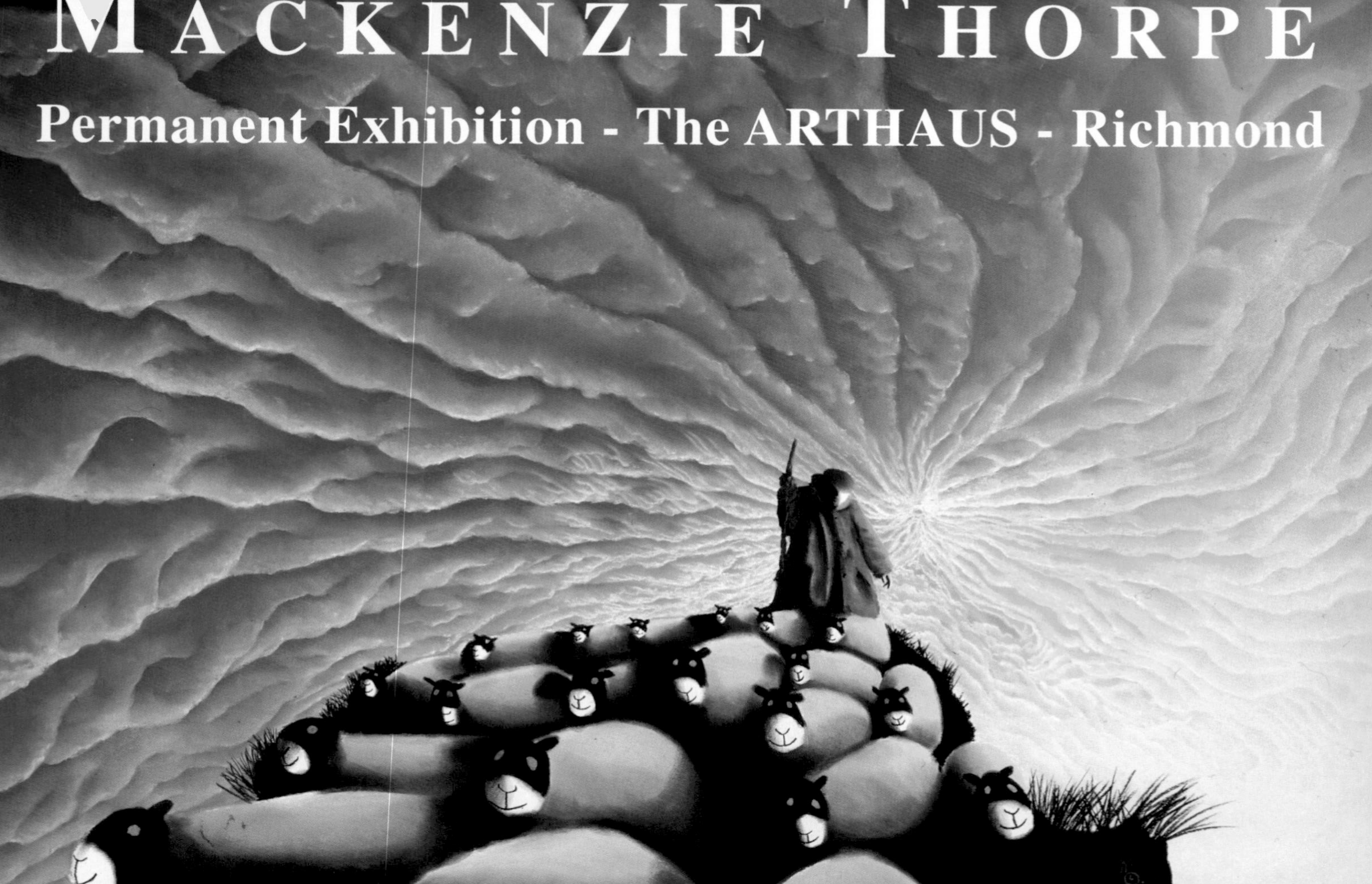
MACKENZIE THORPE
Permanent Exhibition - The ARTHAUS - Richmond

churches, busy with markets and holiday makers, together with some great picture-hunting opportunities. Leyburn has the **Chandler Gallery (01969 623676)**, discreetly hidden just off the main square but providing an attractive selection of some of the region's best artists. If you can tear yourself away from the superb castle at Middleham and stop arguing about whether Richard the Third was really the bad guy history makes him out to be, you will find the **Old School Arts Workshop (01969 623056)** opposite. Exhibitions, bookshop, coffee and cakes – and art courses throughout the summer – make this a valuable outpost for art in a community more famous for its racehorse training establishments.

War and rumour of war made Richmond and its Castle a crucial site for centuries, but now its sloping, arena-like market place is peaceful. Through an archway can be found **The Chapel Gallery (01748 850505)** a busy framer's with a wide selection of prints and originals of local scenes. Nearby, on Rosemary Lane, is **Mackenzie Thorpe's Art Haus (01748 823224)** where the eponymous artist shows his highly individual original drawings and paintings, many with a surreal or amusing flavour, together with prints and cards of the same.

The Gallery at Masham **(01765 689554)** offers an adventurous selection of original art in a tiny gallery that can be found almost in the shadow of the church. A few miles away in Bedale, **The Dales Gallery (01677 423580)** has local prints. In the handsome town of Northallerton, **Hares Studio ((01609 774614)**, off the main thoroughfare, is a framer's with a stock of originals and reproductions, many of which show the town and its environs, including historical prints. Moving south across rich rolling farmland, the **Zillah Bell Gallery (01845 522479)** at Thirsk is a place to enjoy and acquire fine, original contemporary art. Regular exhibitions are accompanied by a wide range of art and crafts. If you decide to head north into County Durham at this point then you should make a bee-line for **The Bowes Museum** at Barnard Castle. Be warned however, you could spend a day in the amazing 19th century French chateau-style museum and still not see all of its collections of fine and decorative art, local history and costume displays.

The north-eastern quarter of our region has so much of beauty and interest that it is hard to imagine anyone having time for gallery-browsing. The lovely, lonely, North Yorkshire moors are stitched with secretive valleys and bordered by the broad Vale of Pickering to the south. Snug Helmsley has yet another castle, and the excellent **Look Gallery (01439 770545)**, while **The Green Man Gallery** at Pickering **(01751 472361)** is a contemporary art bonus to the town's many ancient attractions. Among the most important of these are the 15th century wallpaintings in the Parish Church. **Talents Fine Arts (01653 600020)** at Malton has good original works to suit all tastes.

Among the deep, hidden valleys that crease and dimple the northern edge of the moors, Castleton surprises the visitor with its **Montage Studio Gallery (01287 660159)** which has an adventurous selection of contemporary regional artworks. Eventually, however, the call of the sea takes us all to that most picturesque of Yorkshire fishing ports, Whitby, where the public Art Gallery, **The Pannet Gallery**

(01947 602051), perches above the old town and its harbour. The same scenes, recorded by a famous Victorian Photographer, can be seen in **The Sutcliffe Gallery (01947 602239)** on Flowergate. Down among the seagulls, trippers and fishing boats, the **Penny Hedge Gallery (01947 821310)**, which stocks originals by local artists, prints and cards, can be found on the lane leading up to the Abbey steps, while the **Grape Lane Gallery (no tel.)** is close to the Captain Cook Memorial Museum. In Whitby's old Market Place is **The Studio of John Freeman (01947 602799)**, where visitors can watch a working artist and choose from his watercolours of farms and villages and nocturnal scenes.

Children from nought to ninety head for Scarborough's beaches, but the town has other attractions. There are the diverse historic collections at Scarborough **Art Gallery (01723 374753)**, while **The Stephen Joseph Theatre** has an exhibition area for interesting art.

For the imaginative visitor, walking the streets of York becomes a dramatic living history lesson, and a browse through the superb collections in the **City Art Gallery (01904 551863)** provides an equally fascinating and enjoyable tutorial on art-history through the ages. In the shadow of the Minster, in a tiny back water, **The Stonegate Gallery (01904 635141)** has stimulating exhibitions of a wide range of regional painters, and if contemporary art photography interests you then **Impressions (01904 654724)** near Clifford's Tower should definitely be on your itinerary. On the outskirts of the city **The Kentmere House Gallery (01904 656507)** opens its doors by appointment only – not surprisingly, since it is also a private house.

In the village of Haxby, near the northern ring road, the **Panache Gallery (01904 765333)** has originals by local artists.

Harrogate is quite unique, an elegant spa town which has more of the home counties about it than Yorkshire Grit. The public art gallery, **The Mercer Gallery (01423 503340)**, adds contemporary touring and home-grown exhibitions to changing displays from its interesting public collections. The nearby private **Walker Galleries (01423 567933)** has colourful contemporary works in a traditional manner.

Separated by only a few miles, and often linked with Harrogate, the historic market town of Knaresborough is different again in character. By the Castle Keep, **The Old Courthouse (01423 503340)** museum hosts summer art exhibitions. But for two groups of serious collectors, modest Knaresborough has become a place of pilgrimage. **The Gordon Reece Gallery (01423 866219)** offers a visual feast of exceptional artefacts, particularly textiles, from all over the far and middle East, while **European Ceramics (01423 867401)**, an international player in the world of fine contemporary ceramics, shows pots that are unmistakably serious art.

For those heading for the beautiful ruins of Fountains Abbey, the charming village of Ripley may be a temptation to pause. It attracts many visitors, some of whom find their way into the **Chantry Gallery (01423 771011)** to view the many original works and prints by local artists on display. On the southern edge of the region, on the outskirts of Ilkley, the **Lauron Gallery (01943 600725)** has a selection of prints and originals by local artists, most frequently of Dales and rural scenes, in watercolour and other media.

THE DALES GALLERY

NORTH END, BEDALE

Professional Picture Framing at The Dales Gallery

Originals, Limited Editions, Prints of the dales and a variety of other works

Restoration and Conservation Services

Textiles a speciality

Tuesday – Saturday 10am-5pm
Closed Sunday & Monday
Access & Visa
Tel: 01677 423580

TALENTS FINE ARTS

An outstanding small gallery established 10 years. Filled with highly reputable artists ~ new works constantly on show with a high standard achieved ~ Yorkshire scenes, wildlife and equestrian in all medias. Exhibitions held twice yearly. Visitors welcome to browse.

Open Monday to Saturday 10.00am to 5.00pm

7 Market Place, Malton, N. Yorks. YO17 OLP
Tel: Malton (01653) 600020

The Penny Hedge Gallery

The "Penny Hedge" is Whitby's premier art gallery.

Our extensive stock of original paintings combines the work of the very best local artists with the work of artists from many other parts of Britain.

135, Church Street, Whitby Tel: (01947) 821310

Back to Nature

Courtesy of laurie Campbell

Stretching from the Yorkshire Dales in the west, dipping down into the Vales of Pickering and York and rising again from the North York Moors, North Yorkshire covers some of the richest and most varied wildlife habitats to be found anywhere in Britain.

In the west, limestone dales contrast with the bleak crags of Ingleborough and Pen-Y-Ghent, a landscape with wide vistas, yet full of nooks and crannies crammed with tiny plants and creatures.

To the very north-east, the moors, heather-covered, bleak yet beautiful, roll over to the coast by Scarborough, Filey and Whitby. Here the cliffs attract sea birds by the thousand, whilst every tide exposes fossils that are millions of years old.

In the middle lie the Vales of Pickering and York, rich farmland through which the Rivers Ouse and Derwent wend their way – a countryside of woodlands and hedgerows, ditches and pastures, teeming with wildlife.

THE YORKSHIRE DALES

You can spend a month in the Dales and still see only a fraction of its wildlife. The limestone supports a range of calcium-loving plants, some very rare. The rivers teem with fish, and the summer fields echo to the churring call of the curlew, or the trill of the skylark. Otters are present, though rarely seen, and agriculture still works at a pace that nurtures nature.

Malham Tarn

Go here early in the day, as it is a popular spot for visitors. Surrounded by limestone pavement, this glacial feature is perhaps the best wetland mire in Britain. Cotton grass, marsh marigolds and marsh valerian can be found. In spring, wheatear, curlew, skylark and meadow pipit nest in the fields. On the limestone pavement, a Yorkshire speciality, the grikes, or gaps between the blocks of limestone, create mini-habitats in which grow plants normally associated with woodlands. Dog's mercury, wood anemone and harts-tongue fern are all common.

The Pennine Way takes you to the Tarn from the village. Just before you climb up to the Tarn, Malham Cove appears to block the way, a limestone cliff rising straight in front of you. Here, house martins nest as they did before man provided buildings as substitute cliffs.

Follow the route of Gordale Beck and you pass through wildflower meadows yellow with buttercup. Look closer and there are other colours to be seen: the pink of ragged robin, the blue of meadow cranesbill. This part of Yorkshire holds the finest remnants of meadows created by traditional hay-making.

Ingleborough National Nature Reserve

Ingleborough is a fragile habitat of limestone pavement and mountain landscape. Avoid walking on the limestone pavement – not only is it vulnerable to the steady wear of boots, but it is also dangerous. The grikes between the limestone blocks are deep, and the clints themselves are uneven. However, you can see plenty from the footpath. Solomon's seal, juniper, red helleborine, harts-tongue fern and baneberry nestle between the rocks. Out on the pasture, early purple orchids and primroses can be in flower well into June, long after those further south and nearer sea level have died off.

Higher up the slopes, mountain pansies, bright yellow, grow amongst the grass while roseroot and yellow saxifrage cling to the steep, bare slopes.

River Wharfe

This spectacular river flows quickly down through Wharfedale before turning eastward towards Tadcaster, joining the River Ouse north of Selby.

In the Dales, it is a typical mountain stream. A little rain and it changes to a raging torrent. Dippers, kingfishers, oyster catchers and grey wagtails are regular sights along its upland banks. Lower down, goosanders and heron compete with anglers for the brown and rainbow trout.

The Wharfe is a fine grayling stream, especially in the stretch past Harewood. For the casual visitor, though, a look in one of the many rock pools along the reach by Grassington will reveal not only minnows, but stone loaches too.

There are otters on the Wharfe, but they are rarely seen. On the lower reaches, mink are fairly common, and they can often be spotted in broad daylight.

At Kilnsey Trout Farm, a river-life exhibition has been constructed in an old barn. A series of tanks represent in miniature the various sections of the River Wharfe. For the visitor, it offers a rare chance to see the delights of freshwater life usually hidden from view.

Grassington is a popular watering-hole for thousands of visitors. Close by is Grass Wood, a nature reserve owned and managed by the Yorkshire Wildlife Trust. Next to it is Bastow Wood, a more open habitat in which sheep graze. The list of flowers growing there is enormous but look out for wood sanicle, mountain currant and herb paris in Grass Wood. With patience, you will find lily of the valley, columbine and early purple orchid. Further on, in Bastow Wood there is bird's eye primrose, a pink relative of our other Primula species, along with common and bitter milkwort and mountain everlasting.

Semerwater

Lying in Raydale, not far from Hawes, the glacial lake at Semerwater sits in a spectacular setting. There is a footpath along the eastern side, from Low Blean to Marsett. This takes you past the wetland area on the south western side of the lake.

In summer, a pink blanket of ragged robin covers the west pasture. Marsh cinquefoil, bogbean and both southern and

Courtesy of laurie Campbell

northern marsh orchids grow there too.

On the lake itself, a raft of yellow water-lilies lies close to the edge, whilst a flock of Canada geese is joined by great crested grebe. In winter, whooper swans and widgeon visit the site.

Hares are often seen in the surrounding pastures, and both red and roe deer are occasionally spotted.

Swaledale

Draining the dales to the east is the River Swale. Although there are hay meadows all over the Dales, those alongside the Swale are amongst the best. Still managed in the traditional way, hay is cut late here, so the wildflowers have a chance to blossom and set seed.

As you pass through in late summer, look out for fields purple with wood cranesbill, yellow with buttercups and pink with knapweed, clover and scabious. These are the fields where curlew and lapwings raise their chicks, and brown hares hide their leverets.

After passing through Richmond, the Swale turns south, joining the River Ure, north west of York. The Ure, which rises beyond Hawes in the north-west of the Dales, is yet another Yorkshire river teeming with wildlife. Both the Swale and the Ure have otters living along them, both support populations of native brown trout and both hold colonies of white-clawed crayfish. The banks are home for kingfishers, grey and yellow wagtails, dippers and herons. Oyster catchers fly noisily away as you walk along, but nothing startles you more than the loud piping of common sandpipers, as they fly off, wings beating frantically.

Gouthwaite Reservoir

On the eastern side of the Dales region, this Yorkshire Water Services nature reserve has a car park with viewing point which is noted for sightings of birds of prey. Every autumn and early in the year, birds such as golden eagle, rough-legged buzzard and common buzzard can be seen as they pass through.

Red kites, which have been increasing in numbers as a result of a successful captive breeding programme, have also been seen in recent years. One cannot guarantee any particular bird on a given day, but local people usually know what is about.

Fountains Abbey

Although this is an artificial landscape in many ways, the influence of man has enabled a whole range of wild flowers to find a home here. Others have been brought along on purpose, perhaps as herbs and medicines for the monks.

Common pink and wallflower decorate the walls, as do pellitory-of-the-wall, harebell, storksbill, golden rod and blue fleabane.

By the old water courses you will find butterbur and monkey flower, skullcap, marsh marigold, water avens and marsh valerian. In the water itself are white water lily, water crowfoot, water mint and spiked water milfoil.

It is the woodlands bordering the grounds that harbour the real rarity. Amongst the beech grows bird's nest orchid. A strange looking plant, it has no chlorophyll and flowers in the darkest of woods. In colour it looks pinky-brown and it stands about 30cms high.

Don't worry if you can't find the orchid. Spend your time looking for greater bellflower, enchanter's nightshade and deadly nightshade, yellow pimpernel and mountain currant.

NORTH YORK MOORS

The moors are drained to the south by the Rivers Rye, Seph, Dove and Seven. Together with Hodge Beck they swell the River Derwent as it flows from Forge Valley down through Pickering and Malton and along the Vale of York.

To the north, flowing eastward to Whitby, the River Esk is one of the few English rivers where salmon can be seen leaping up the falls to their spawning grounds. The moors themselves are covered not only with ling, the most common heather, but with bell heather and, in wet patches, cross-leaved heath. Crowberry and cowberry grow in patches, and, when the drainage is poor, bogs are created in which cotton grass, cranberry, bog-myrtle, and bog rosemary may grow.

Emperor moths can be seen on the wing, while grouse are a common sight. However, as you walk along, look carefully at the ground. On the lower slopes, adders and common lizards can be seen, basking on the sandy soils.

Farndale

In spring, this nature reserve, owned by the North York Moors National Park, is ablaze with wild daffodils. Growing by the banks of the River Dove, they may have originally been planted by monks. Now they are protected by law and it is an offence to dig them up, or even pick them. "Take only photographs, leave only footprints" is a sound code by which to travel our countryside.

Forge Valley Woods

A National Nature Reserve, owned by English Nature, this is a rich woodland site. In spring, primrose, bluebells, wood anemones, wood sorrel and early purple

orchid give way to strong smelling wild ramsons later on.

The trees include oak, ash and elm, with alder and willow in the damp areas of the valley bottom. Hazel, holly, hawthorn, elder and rowan make up the understorey. Summer visiting birds, such as chiff-chaff, wood and willow warblers, join the residents, such as nuthatch and great spotted woodpecker. This is a wood to take your picnic to.

Levisham Moor

A large reserve of 2,000 acres owned by North York Moors National Park, Levisham Moor covers a wide range of habitats. On the moorland, you can find bilberry and crowberry, tormentil, heath bedstraw and sheeps sorrel. The birds include curlew, red grouse, snipe, golden plover and meadow pipit.

Woodlands on the edge of the moors contain small-leaved lime, guelder rose, field maple and scots pine. Bluebells and primrose carpet the ground in Spring, while Roe deer slip quietly through the trees and out into the pastures to graze early in the mornings.

THE EAST COAST

Apart from the obvious attractions of fish and chips, ice cream and a paddle in the sea, the coast is a haven for wildlife. Perhaps more importantly, it is home for an entirely different range of species.

The steep cliffs of the East Coast offer safe nesting sites for thousands of sea birds, from fulmars and kittiwakes, to puffins and guillemots. Above the picturesque village of Staithes, a large breeding colony of herring gulls occupies the cliff top. Do not venture into these sites, as the parents are very protective – and noisy. Keep well away from the cliff edges, as winds, vertigo, or loose soil could easily prove your downfall.

Down on the beach there is a different world. Search the strand line of washed up seaweed after the tide has receded and you may find edible crabs, shore crabs, razor shells, mussels, urchins, and starfish. Where there are rock pools, look for prawns, shrimps and flat winkles. This part of the county is one of the few places where the spiny squat lobster lives, hidden under stones. On sandy beaches, the masked crab, which is straw-coloured, hides in the sand by day, like shrimps do. Look out also for the thornback or spiny spider crab.

Fossil-rich rock occurs all the way down to Scarborough, and includes Robin Hood's Bay. Below Scarborough, younger rocks form the coastline, but at Filey Brigg, especially on the north side, fossil-bearing rocks again emerge and a wide selection can easily be found.

VALES OF PICKERING AND YORK

The Dales and Moors National Parks cover the uplands of North Yorkshire, but between them are two vales through which the River Derwent flows on its way to meet the River Ouse. Dominated by excellent agricultural land, the Vales contain the sort of wildlife you expect on farmland. Brown hares, fox, badger, partridge and skylark are typical of the area. However, the Vales also forms the flood plain of the River Derwent and Ouse. These in turn produce wetlands, marshes and open waters. This type of habitat has reduced in abundance over the past fifty years. Drainage for agriculture and development of new roads and housing have all had an impact. Fortunately, a few remnants remain, owned and managed by wildlife conservation groups and organisations, or just retained by sympathetic landowners.

Askham Bog

On the very outskirts of York, alongside the A64, this 120 acre nature reserve has a special place in wildlife history. It was the first nature reserve bought by the Yorkshire Wildlife Trust, and in fact it was the purchase of this site which prompted its formation in 1946. It is regarded by many as one of the best wetland nature reserves in the country.

The plants to be seen include royal fern and water violet, bog myrtle and alder buckthorn. This last shrub is the food plant to the larvae of the brimstone butterfly, a lovely sulphur-yellow butterfly which is on the wing early in spring, with a second generation in late summer. For those who love mammals, water voles and roe deer are regularly seen, while rabbits abound. In late spring and throughout the summer, the trees and shrubs are alive with birdsong. The summer visitors include grasshopper warbler, willow warbler, chiff-chaff, blackcap and whitethroat.

Wheldrake Ings

Forming part of the Lower Derwent Ings National Nature Reserve, Wheldrake, again owned by the Yorkshire Wildlife Trust, comprises 400 acres of flood meadow on the River Derwent, bounded to the north by the old course of the river, on the west by the river itself and to the east and south by the Pocklington Canal.

In winter, when the river floods, thousands of wildfowl seek refuge on the reserve. Bewick swan, greylag and brent geese, teal, pochard and widgeon visit in huge flocks. Come the summer, and wading birds, such as lapwing, redshank, snipe and curlew nest in the long grass of the hay meadows.

Courtesy of Pete Bowler

Still managed as they were in Saxon times, the wet hay meadows are an important feature of Wheldrake Ings. Full of meadowsweet, great burnet, meadow cranesbill and pepper saxifrage, the fields are a riot of colour until mown in mid-July. Farmers from far and wide bid for the right to cut hay from field allotments marked out by boundary stones at the edges.

Butterflies feeding on the flowers, include the small copper, whilst dragonflies and damselflies hunt for their insect prey. The beautiful banded agrion damselfly, a deep emerald green in colour, is a common sight.

Bolton-on-Swale Lakes

Further north, this nature reserve is one of the few expanses of open water in Richmondshire. Situated close to the River Swale and the A1, this onetime gravel-pit covers some 27 acres, and in winter is a haven for wildfowl, such as teal, widgeon and tufted ducks.

Skipwith Common

Not all the wildlife sites in the Vale of York are wetlands. At Skipwith Common, 600 acres of dry heath, woodland and some marsh, provide one of the most important lowland heath sites in the North.

In summer, ground-nesting birds, such as the very rare nightjar, make it necessary for visitors to stick to footpaths. Nightjars are on the wing in the late dusk, feeding on moths and other insects.

There are orchids at Skipwith; twayblade, and broad-leaved helleborine. Yellow-wort grows by the old concrete runways, part of a World War II bomber airfield, whilst the heath is covered in ling heather. A small patch of marsh gentian, an autumn flowering, deep blue flower, lies tucked away in one corner and the rare pill-wort grows in a newly created pond. Common lizards and adders can be spotted basking in the sunshine, but the herd of fallow deer is rarely seen.

The new pond, created close to the King Rudding Road entrance at Riccall, supports both frog and toad populations. In early spring the background chorus of croaking will guide you to where it is.

Strensall Common

Six miles north of York lies the village of Strensall, on the outskirts of which, on the Flaxton Road, lies Strensall Common. Purchased by the Yorkshire Wildlife Trust from the Ministry of Defence in 1979, it covers 105 acres of lowland heath. Some beautiful flowers are to be found here, including marsh cinquefoil, marsh gentian and sundew. From these you will know that the heath is not dry all year round. Indeed, there are usually large areas of open water, so you will need your wellies.

Not everyone is fascinated by insects, but Strensall is worth visiting for its purple hairstreak butterflies, bog bush crickets and glow-worms.

Take care as you walk along, because adders often bask on the open ground. Common lizards can be seen, and the mammals include fox, brown hare and harvest mouse.

Period Pieces

Often the best way to impress is to conceal, theatrically revealing your treasures to an admiring audience. And so it is with many of Yorkshire's finest architectural masterpieces – most are hidden from the casual gaze.

Harewood House (0113 2886331) is home to the Queen's cousin, the Earl of Harewood and his family. Princess Mary, his mother, lived here from 1929 until her death in 1965.

Complementing Carr's Palladian architecture, Harewood is filled with rarities – art-works by Titian, Turner and Gainsborough, furniture specially made for the house by Chippendale, and exquisite Adam plasterwork. The house, however, is just one facet of your visit. **Harewood Bird Garden** displays a living, often noisy collection, whose feathered inhabitants are every bit as exotic as the objects on show indoors. Stroll among 1,000 acres of tranquil landscaped grounds down to the lake with its own steam launch, or visit the newly-restored South Terrace parterres. Capability Brown might have raised an eyebrow at the huge adventure playground. A magnet to children, it is one of the best in the county.

Although much older, **Ripley Castle (01423 770152)**, like its grander neighbour, forms the centrepiece of an estate-designed 'model' village. Like Harewood, it boasts outstanding pleasure grounds, parkland walks and gardens, which include the National Hyacinth Collection. The fine paintings and heirlooms within these Gothic walls tell a story of warfare and religious persecution, through 28 generations of the Ingilby family.

Not far away, the great tower and soaring arches of **Fountains Abbey (01765 608888)** reflected in the calm waters of the Skell combine to produce the finest and most picturesque monastic ruin in the country. Built by the Cistercians whose business acumen brought the Abbey immense riches, it was later adopted by Sir John Aislaby of neighbouring **Studley Royal**. In his passion for gardening, he transformed the grounds into a classic 18th century confection of landscaped drives and follies, with the ruined Abbey a breathtaking finale for his guests.

Completing a trio of gems close to Harrogate is **Newby Hall (01423 322583)**, alterations to which were expressly made to accommodate its owner's holiday souvenirs! Taking 'The Grand Tour' in the 1760s, William Weddell returned with a splendid collection of classical Italian statuary and a complete set of specially commissioned Gobelin Tapestries. The stunning rooms designed by Robert Adam show them off to perfection.

Simple, dignified and restrained, **Beningbrough Hall (01904 470666)**, completed in 1716, is Georgian – slightly later than its Jacobean counterpart at **Sheriff Hutton (01347 878442)**. Beningbrough Hall changed hands several times before passing to the National Trust in 1959 in payment of death duties. Major restoration and the loan of portraits from the National Gallery have given the house a new lease of life, but it is the fine woodwork, including a superb oak staircase, which arouse most admiration.

Aristocratic lifestyles would not have been possible had they not been underpinned by an army of servants. At Ben-

ingbrough, the Victorian Laundry and Potting Shed demonstrate the reality of working life for those employed 'below stairs'. If you picture yourself as one of the nobility however, you might book ahead and attend a soirée at Sheriff Hutton, where the costumed actors of the East 15 Company will welcome you to their productions of Shakespearean and Jacobean plays.

Almost hidden by trees, you'll see the domed cupola of Yorkshire's largest house long before you reach it. Set in 1,000 acres of grounds, **Castle Howard (01653 648444)**, six miles west of Malton, was the vision of the 3rd Earl of Carlisle, whose descendants still live here. Built in the style of Wren to plans by the then unknown Vanbrugh, it cost over £78,000 and was 37 years under construction. By 1737, when it was finished, both Earl and architect were dead. Their legacy, however, is remarkable for its lavishness and beauty. Epitomising the age of gracious living, Castle Howard was a natural choice for the filming of *Brideshead Revisited.*

At nearby Helmsley, Palladian **Duncombe Park (01439 770213)** overlooks the open expanses of the North York Moors. Following the death of the 2nd Earl at the Battle of the Somme, the house languished for almost 70 years as a girls' school. But in 1985, the present Lord and Lady Feversham returned to the family seat and began its painstaking restoration. The results accurately portray a variety of styles popular in the 18th and 19th centuries. Thanks to the judicious use of family paintings and furniture, it is hard to believe that a mere ten years ago Duncombe Park was little more than an empty shell.

Late 17th century **Nunnington Hall (01439 748283)** stands beside the River Rye, close to a picturesque packhorse bridge. It was tenanted in the 16th century by Robert Huickes, physician to Henry VIII, Edward VI and Elizabeth I, a doctor who had the unenviable task of informing Her Majesty that she could never have children. Inside, a magnificent oak-panelled hall leads to cosy family rooms, servants quarters and attics which look much as they did when the last owners gave it to the National Trust in 1952. One of its most remarkable features is the Carlisle Collection of Miniature Rooms. More than mere dolls' furniture, these unique set-pieces began with one woman's fascination with all things tiny. As her collection grew she commissioned craftsmen to build one-eighth sized rooms in which to display them, ultimately donating the results to the National Trust.

You'll find there are walls within walls in York. The city's encircling ramparts enclose the walled garden of the **Treasurer's House (01904 624247)**, sheltering by the towering **Minster**. Considered by some to be the most beautiful building in York, it dates from the 1620's and yields up a wealth of period furniture, china and antique glass. But this property will leave you with more questions than answers. Why, for example, did its last owner, Frank Green, put brass studs in the floors of its magnificent rooms? And are the stories of ghostly Roman soldiers tramping knee-high through the cellar really true?

On The Line

At the cross-roads of North Yorkshire, Thirsk is a superb angling centre. The Cod Beck flows through the town and holds prolific stocks of coarse fish, together with a good head of trout and grayling. Nearby, the delightful rivers Swale and Ure provide good trout and grayling fishing, their lower reaches offering excellent sport for barbel, chub, roach, dace, perch and pike. For both stillwater game and coarse anglers there is a wide choice of local lakes. Further afield are many small river and stream venues for those seeking the romance of wilder places.

A few hundred yards west of Thirsk town centre, on the corner of Sowerby Road, you can find the **Thirsk Anglers Centre (01845 524684)**, one of the best tackle shops in the north of England. Proprietors Pat and Derek Stratton stock a comprehensive range of rods, reels, flies and accessories from all over the world. Derek, a passionate angler, an accomplished fly-tier and a national fly-fishing instructor, gives expert tuition in all aspects of game fishing for trout and salmon.

The following list of fishing venues recommended by Derek is divided conveniently between trout and coarse fishing options. Trout fishing is obviously the more expensive, but day tickets, even at the most popular trout lakes represent excellent value for money, when you take into account opportunities for fish suppers. Coarse fishing, on the other hand, can be had for a few pounds, and many of our northern rivers contain specimen barbel and chub – dour, tackle-breaking fish which so typify Yorkshire pluck. Buy extra rods!

TROUT FISHING

Wykeham Lakes, Charm Park, Scarborough (01723 863148) Fly fishing for specimen rainbow and brown trout on three beautifully landscaped, spring-fed lakes. Season from March to October. Day and evening tickets. A fourth lake (open all year) is available for small dingy sailing, windsurfing, canoeing and scuba diving. Ample space for walking, and picnicking for non-angling members of the family. *Wykeham Lakes are south of the A170 Scarborough to Pickering road.*

Scalby Beck, Scarborough. Flowing through a partly-wooded, sinuous ravine whose open banks are a riot of flowers in summer, the largely undiscovered beck debouches into Scarborough's North Bay at Scalby Mills. Cascades and glides, fly fishing for brown trout and occasional sea trout. Excellent for family picnics. *Access to the lower reaches is via a footpath immediately above the Scalby Mills Hotel. The upstream footpath is below the Burniston Road bridge on the A165 road to Whitby.*

Rivers Rye and Seph, Hawnby (tel. the Hawnby Hotel on 01439 798202) Wild headwaters trout fishing, surrounded by glorious moorland scenery, resident fishing only. *Hawnby is west of the B1257 Helmsley to Stokesley road.*

River Esk at Danby and Castleton (tel. Danby Post Office on 01287 660220 and Castleton Post Office on 01287 660201) A fabled river with its outlet in Whitby, providing trout and, when water levels are reasonable, autumnal sea-trout and occasional salmon fishing on the Egton Estates stretches. *Danby and Castleton are south of the A171 Whitby to Guisborough road.*

Low Osgoodby Lake, near Thirsk (01845 597601) Under the gaze of the famous White Horse of Kilburn, this two-acre lake offers good rainbow trout fishing and is suitable for disabled anglers. *Close to Sutton Bank, the lake is just south of the Thirsk to Helmsley road between Balk and Kilburn.*

Cod Beck, Thirsk (tel. Thirsk Angling Centre on 01845 524684) Lush meadows, small stream brown trout and grayling fishery (stocked). Ideally suited to the roving style. *Access is north of the town.*

Raker Lakes, Wheldrake (01904 448793) Nearly three acres of trout fishing and two separate coarse lakes stocked with carp, bream, tench, roach and perch. *Conveniently close to York (south-east). Take the B1228 from the A64 Grimston roundabout east of the city and go due south just before Elvington.*

Farmire Trout Fishery, Farnham, Knaresborough (01423 866417) A former quarry splendidly transformed into a five acre lake and nature reserve. Rare flowers and birds, rainbow and brown trout up to 10lbs. Barbless hooks only. Advisable to book ahead. Two boats. Open all year. Day and evening tickets. Facilities for disabled anglers. *North of Harrogate. Take the B6165 from Knaresborough or from the A61 roundabout at Ripley and turn north through Scotton for 1.5 miles.*

Leighton Reservoir, Swinton, near Masham (01765 689024) In a wild moorland setting at 750 feet above sea level, this 105-acre trout fishery has the majesty of a Scottish loch. Rainbows in the 4lb range are plentiful, together with a fair sprinkling of brown trout. Open during the trout season. Day and evening tickets are available from the fishing cabin on the west side of the reservoir. *Take the A6108 to Masham and go west for 4 miles through the villages of Fearby and Healey, forking left downhill to the reservoir.*

River Skirfare, Arncliffe, Littondale (tel. Falcon Inn on 01756 770205) In stunning scenery, four miles of wild trout and grayling fishing on a tributary of the Wharfe. Day tickets: fly only. No Sunday fishing. Best from May onwards. *Go north from Grassington on the B6160, pass Kilnsey Crag, and after about 4 miles fork left into Arncliffe.*

River Ure (upper reaches) - (tel. the Board Hotel, Hawes on 01969 667223 and Lowis Countrywear, Hawes 01969 667443) Trout and grayling fishing in upper Wensleydale with freedom to fish the tributary becks – Hardraw, Cotter, Mossdale, Widdale and Duerley. Both fly and bait fishing are allowed. *The river is in the Yorkshire Dales National Park and can be accessed from the A684. There are numerous fishery access points – details from the ticket distributors.*

Kilnsey Park Lake, Kilnsey (01756 752150) In the heart of the Dales overlooked by the imposing 170ft eminence of Kilnsey Crag, two ponds stocked with rainbow trout to an incredible 20 pounds. Fun fishery for young children, a trout farm shop, a large aquarium, adjoining Daleslife Visitor Centre and refreshment and picnic facilities. Open all year. Day and half-day permits. *The fishery is just off the B6160 Skipton to Kettlewell road, north of Grassington.*

Tanfield Lodge, West Tanfield (01677 470385) A picturesque seven-and-a-half-acre former gravel pit up to 30 feet deep. Challenging fly fishing for brown and rainbow trout in gin-clear water. Good fly hatches. Small flies and light tackle recommended. Fishing hut and car park. *West Tanfield is north-west of Ripon on the A6108. After crossing the Ure, turn left through the village and go left at the next bend down an unmade road.*

Thornton Steward Reservoir, Bedale (tel. Finghall Post Office on 01677 450245) In pleasant countryside, a generously stocked brown and rainbow trout fishery and sailing lake. The western bay is reserved exclusively for anglers. Barbless hooks only. Day and evening tickets. *Thornton Steward is mid-way between Bedale and Leyburn south of the A684.*

COARSE FISHING

River Swale - Marske and Richmond Areas (tel. Gilsan Sports, Richmond on 01748 822108) In an historic area studded with ancient castles, abbeys and priories, some 15 scenic miles of trout and grayling *(from Marske Bridge above Richmond)* and dace, chub and barbel fishing *(below Richmond to Brompton on Swale)*. No spinning.

Woodland Lakes, Carlton Miniott (01845 522827 or 0831 824870) A complex of man-made lakes, well stocked with a variety of fish. Permits available bankside. *The lakes are just west of Thirsk and north of the A61.*

Kay's Lakes, Sessay (01845 501321) An excellent quality mixed fishery based on three new lakes. *The lakes are south of Thirsk. Access via the A168 and Dalton or the A19 and Hutton Sessay.*

Welham Lake, Malton (01751 473101) Five acres of woodland-fringed tench fishing – the best in Yorkshire, with 100lb catches not uncommon. Also carp. Bread flake on size ten hooks fished near weedbeds is productive. Only eight rods allowed. Advanced booking essential. *The lake is on the outskirts of Malton. Take the Welham Road and follow the golf club signs.*

Castle Howard Lake, Castle Howard (01653 648331) Eyed by the monumental Castle Howard, this is surely one of the grandest fishing venues in England. A

specimens lake for tench, bream, roach, odd perch and huge pike (record 43 lbs 8oz). Swing-tip ledgering and waggler popular. Tickets from the bankside bailiff. *From Barton Hill on the A64 between York and Malton go due north on the spectacular access road.*

Semerwater Lake, Countersett, Near Hawes (01969 650295/650436) Feeding the River Bain – the shortest in Yorkshire – this reed-fringed 100-acre natural lake is surrounded by spectacular scenery. Bream abound, (swimfeeder tactics recommended) together with roach, perch and wild brown trout. The lake is open to water skiers on Mondays, Tuesdays, Wednesdays and Sundays. Excellent walking country. Tickets available from Low Blean Farm, next to the lake. *Semerwater is in the Yorkshire Dales National Park, 2.5 miles south-east of Bainbridge on the A684 Hawes – Leyburn road.*

Malham Tarn, Field Studies Centre, Malham (01729 830331) Owned by the National Trust, at 1200 feet above sea level, the most beautifully situated of Yorkshire's natural lakes, containing Loch Leven trout and specimen perch. Fishing from boats, fly and worm allowed. *Malham is north-west of Skipton. Go north from the A65 at Coniston Cold.*

Sponsored by Thirsk Anglers Centre

Having a Field Day

North Yorkshire offers a huge variety of opportunities for country sports enthusiasts. It is hardly surprising therefore, that it also boasts a good range of specialist shops offering the kinds of clothing and equipment which devotees of the outdoor life will find essential. Here are five of the very best — each of which can provide specialist advice and many happy hours of browsing.

When Betty Carter set up her country clothing shop in the centre of Helmsley 20 years ago, little did she know that it would become internationally famous. **Carters Countrywear** customers come from all over the world and even has members of the Royal Family and scores of European aristocrats on its mailing list. As its name suggests, Carters, which is still a family business, specialises in clothing connected with country pursuits and stocks all the best brands – Schoffel jackets, Viyella shirts, Rockport shoes. But it is the made-to-measure service which has helped make Carters renowned. The tailoring section sends shooting suits and hand-knitted shooting socks to Australia, America and all over Europe. Country lovers will also be hard-pressed to resist the rare and unusual giftware.

Carters Countrywear at 7 Market Place, Helmsley, is open 9.30am-5.30pm Mon-

4

Sat and 10.30am-5.30pm Sun. Tel. 01439 770688

York's ancient, winding streets are home to some of the most interesting, individual outlets in the country. Many, like the wonderful **Ellerker's,** are located in Walmgate. The shop, which recently celebrated its 200th anniversary, has a historic timbered front which promises character – and visitors aren't left disappointed. They are greeted by the smell of leather and the sight of oak panelling and beams. At the far end of the shop, chairs are gathered around a fireplace. Country lovers might think they have died and gone to heaven. The stock includes Barbour, John Partridge and shoes from Loakes and Allan & Caswell. The best European brands such as Blicker and Schneider are on the shelves, plus hats, scarves, leather and canvas bags and, of course, the best fleeces. Ellerker's also pride themselves on having everything for the equestrian.

Ellerker's of York is at 25 Walmgate. Open 9am-5.30pm Mon-Sat. Tel. 01904 654417

Amongst Middleham's many claims to fame was the late trainer Captain Crump, who was responsible for training three Grand National winners. One of the most exciting new developments in the town is sited in Crump's old premises, Warwick House. **Race Riders** supplies both the racing industry and members of the public. It concentrates on clothing and footwear, with everything from silks to Musto waterproof clothing. It also has an embroidery machine with patterns for scores of logos and which can also "do anything with words".

Race Riders of Warwick House, Middleham is open Tues-Sat 9am-5pm and 10am- 4pm Sun. Tel. 01969 624797.

Real saddlers are few and far between, so it is a real treat to find one in the quaint market town of Wetherby, which itself has a fine racing tradition. The saddling part of **Yorkshire Riding Supplies** has been established for 200 years, and has survived where many have disappeared. The shop, now on Northgate, expanded ten years ago and sells everything from walking and riding clothing to tack, pet equipment and feed. The saddlers also carry out repairs to saddles and bridles.

Yorkshire Riding Supplies on Northgate, Wetherby. Open Mon-Fri 8.45am-5.45pm and Sat 8.45-5.30pm. Tel: 01937 586070.

Edward Kendall turned a treasured hobby into a thriving business 12 years ago. Despite the recent rash of bad publicity surrounding shooting, it continues to thrive – thanks to a loyal band of sportsmen and women who know there is no substitute for real passion and in-depth knowledge. Tucked away at the rear of Long Street, Easingwold, **Shooting Services** is very much a family firm. Run alongside the joinery business by Mr Kendall, his daughter Marnie, and his son Philip, it sells everything from shotguns and air rifles to country clothing and accessories. It also undertakes weapon repairs, and even offers passport-size photographs for use on gun licences.

Shooting Services is at the rear of 180-182 Long Street, Easingwold. Open Mon-Fri 9am-5pm and Sat 9am-3.30pm. Tel. 01347 821356.

Inside Story

In most towns the 'here today, gone tomorrow' culture of retailing has taken over. Fortunately there are still a few traditional family firms – and newer ventures – where you can always be sure of getting something beautiful and unusual with which to enhance your home.

Harrisons of Ripon, in the centre of the market town, has been a family concern since it was established in 1836, and its many years in business are a testament to the quality of its wares. It sells some of the best gift and tableware, including Royal Doulton, Ainsley and Minton. The china department specialises in the highly collectable Border Fine Arts figures and Country Artists models. The printing and stationery side of the business is still strong, and tapestries are a speciality. The shop prides itself on service and the staff are long-serving, knowledgeable and committed to good, old-fashioned customer care.
Harrisons of Ripon, 4 Market Place, Ripon, open 9am-5.30pm Mon-Sat. Tel. 01765 602127

One fledgling business which is sure to be around for many years to come is **Pinetiques** in Thirsk. Started by cabinet makers Stuart Graham and Chris Carney three years ago, it is a million miles away from the mass-produced pine furniture which has swamped the market recently. Stuart and Chris are masters of their craft, and one look at their wares reveals the quality and care which is their trademark. "It is made properly, not just nailed together," says Chris. Pinetiques design, make and fit kitchens and bedrooms, and will create made to measure furniture to specific requirements. Of their standard ranges, sturdy farmhouse tables are most popular. Definitely the antiques of the future.
Pinetiques is at 2 Finkle Street, Thirsk, open Mon-Sat 9.30am-5pm, except Wednesday. Tel. 01845 522177.

Anyone who has visited Indonesia will have marvelled at the beauty and quality of the craftsmanship. **Eastern Origins** in Richmond brings the best of Balinese and Javanese craftwork under one roof. Owner Darren Sydall decided to open his own outlet after spending two years selling Indonesian furniture in Hong Kong for a large company. "Indonesian furniture is different, fabulous quality," he says, "but because of the Dutch influence in the Far East, it appeals to European tastes." The shop sells everything from settees, Roman seats, mirrors and bookcases to tables and medicine cabinets. Prices are keen too, from candles costing a matter of pence to furniture up to £700.
Eastern Origins is at 2 New Road, Richmond, open Mon-Sat 9.30am-5.30pm and Sunday 11am-4pm. Tel. 01748 822339.

French House Antiques is the sort of find that you want to keep to yourself for purely selfish reasons. When friends ask where you got that chic chaise longue, you will be loath to divulge your secret. The shop is crammed with treasures from across the Channel. Collecting French antiques began as a hobby for the Hazells, who soon began selling their finds to the trade. Their first retail venture is sure to capture the imagination of discerning home owners. They specialise in provincial furniture and have everything from beds and wardrobes to refurbished roll-top baths and carved radiators. They also have kitchen paraphernalia and doors, balconies and balustrades stripped from old hotels in the South West of France. The prices are very keen — from £350 for a double bed and £400 for a roll top bath.
French House Antiques are at 74 Micklegate, York, open Mon-Sat 10am-5pm. Tel: 01904 624465.

If you want to invest in a fine oriental rug, then you will find nowhere better than **Dennis Yorke** in Haxby, near York. This fabulous shop is acknowledged as one of the leaders in the field of oriental rugs and carpets, and the advice and help on offer there is invaluable. For instance, did you know, that a rug's colours are symbolic, with red meaning success and yellow representing riches and glory? There are over 3,000 rugs and carpets in stock, and carpets can be made to customers' own designs. Dennis Yorke also undertake repairs, restoration and cleaning of carpets, rugs and kilims.

Dennis Yorke is at 24 The Village, Haxby and is open Mon-Sat 9am-5.30pm. Tel. 01904 769689.

Visitors to **Fox's Pine**, Easingwold can relax in the knowledge that the pine furniture sold here is all genuinely antique. "Nothing reclaimed or made up" is how owner Judith Fox describes it. Instead, beautifully delicate Georgian drawing room furniture stands beside the more robust kitchenalia from Victorian times. This shop is a real treat for lovers of pine and other genuinely old country furniture in oak and yew.

Fox's Pine is at 108 Long Street, Easingwold and is open Mon-Sat 10am-5pm. Closed Thursday. Tel. 01347 822977

Duo in Richmond is one of those shops that is a feast for the eyes. Run by sisters Dale and Rhona, Duo, which is just off the market square, was established three years ago. "Rhona and I are both chefs," says Dale, "but we were looking for a new business and we thought there was a need for a gift shop which was a bit different." Duo's stock is stylish and very design-led. It includes silk and dried flowers, cards, wooden plaques, ceramic mirrors, chrome kitchenware and hand-painted glassware.

Duo is on Newbiggin, Richmond. It opens Mon-Sat 9.30am-5.30pm and Sun 1pm-5pm. Tel. 01748 850614.

A Mecca for home-makers, interior designers and collectors world-wide, the bi-monthly **Great Northern International Antiques Fair (01325 380077)**, is a grand day out. With a permanent home on Harrogate's Great Yorkshire Showground, summer events regularly attract 10,000 visitors to browse among almost 400 indoor and outdoor stands. A riot of colour and activity, here you'll find everything from clocks and 'kitchenalia' to furniture and textiles displayed, with prices starting at under £5. Admission to the three-day Fairs is £3.50 on Fridays (12am-6pm) and £2.75 on Saturdays and Sundays (9.30am-5pm), with excellent group facilities for coach parties.

With antiques, authenticity is all. So, whether buying or selling, it's best to consult the experts. Who better to ask than top London auctioneers and valuers, **Bonhams**, whose nerve centre for their northern network of regional offices is at 14 Market Place, Bedale (01677 424114). Building on the firm's 200 year-old reputation for fine art, specialist and sporting sales, Henrietta Graham and her team of professionals are on hand in Bedale to give free saleroom valuations and advice on forthcoming sales, nation-wide. Drop in to leaf through their massive and up-to-date selection of catalogues and if something catches your eye, Bonhams will happily send bids down for you too.

Sponsored by Bradford & Bingley Building Society.

Made in Yorkshire

Courtesy of P. Chan & C. Abbott

Given a strong tradition of rural creativity and abundant natural resources, it is hardly surprising that Yorkshire boasts a wide range of crafts. Nor is it surprising that many of these products enjoy a world-wide market, for they are imbued not only with their makers' artistic gifts but with a real passion for the surroundings which inspired them. Many workshops welcome visitors, but it is always a good idea to phone ahead. Often craftspeople work alone and their opening hours can be erratic.

In Ryedale, **Brookfield Rugs** near Coxwold **(01347 868321)** encompasses all the ideals of Yorkshire thriftiness. Barbara Robson designs and makes authentic, hessian-backed, "clippy" rag rugs from wools and cottons, often gleaned from jumble sales. Colourful, creative and fun, these warm rugs have something of the Victorian country cottage about them – quite unlike anything you'll find on the High Street. Barbara has a large collection of original designs for sale, or will work to your specifications to create a unique and eye-catching heirloom of your very own.

Retired BBC News Editor, Vin Bootle, is now better known for his jewellery. Working from his home near **Boroughbridge (01423 324108)**, Vin's interest in history inspired his best-known design, which is based on the ancient decorative pattern called 'Celtic Weave'. Though it appears on many ancient artefacts, Vin was the first to adapt it to metal. The result: highly unusual bracelets and rings formed from strands of silver, which catch both the light and the eye.

Visit Vin on summer weekends at Helmsley's regular **Town Hall Craft Fair** and you'll be well-placed to discover **The Toy Shop** in Meeting House Court **(01439 771020)**. A friendly, old fashioned toy shop where everything is built to last. A working train steams round the window, while inside tractors and teddies rub shoulders with farmyards and assorted hand-finished sturdy wooden toys, limited edition toys and collectables. Large toys to order. Worldwide postal service available.

There's handmade furniture to admire in the tiny hamlet of Balk, nearby. At the **Old Mill (01845 597227)** a team of specialist craftsmen choose just the right pieces of carefully-seasoned hardwood for

their modern and traditional designs. The extensive portfolio includes pieces crafted in oak, walnut, maple, mahogany, cherry, elm, chestnut and ash.

Also on display at The Old Mill is Moorcroft Pottery and other craft items.

Don't pass through Easingwold, on the A19 between Thirsk and York, without stopping off to visit **Snowden's Jewellery Workshop (01347 822962)** at 95 Long Street. From here, Mark and Alison Snowden have supplied top-class work to outlets throughout the United Kingdom over the course of the last five years. Mark particularly enjoys making gold rings, and one of his specialities is designing one-off wedding rings to fit snugly with the prospective wearer's engagement ring. He also works with silver and precious stones, and is happy to make pretty much any piece to the commissioner's specifications. Independent jewellers are increasingly rare nowadays, so it is always encouraging to find a genuine craftsman who deals directly with the public.

Finding the workshops of **Jorvik Glass (01653 648555)** couldn't be easier, as they are located in the stable yard of Castle Howard, one of Yorkshire's largest and grandest houses.

Watch spellbound as Angela Henderson coaxes a molten ball of glass into objects of great beauty before your eyes. Both commissions and her own distinctive functional and decorative creations are made in the traditional way and are on display in the gift shop, where colourful ornaments glint and sparkle alongside elegant wine glasses and decanters fine enough even to grace the table of Castle Howard itself.

East, towards the coast, the dappling sunlight, ever-changing clouds and the misty Vale of York provide subjects for Richard Keeton. Find his studio at **Holly House,** West Lutton **(01944 738520)**, and you'll be rewarded by the brilliance of Richard's etchings and water colours. Strong, interesting work, using both figurative and abstract styles, his paintings are increasingly sought after. His haunting and evocative images will stay with you long after you have left the studio.

Reflecting the seaside high-spirits of lively Scarborough, the sign above the door of **Step-To Crafts,** Wykeham **(01723 865212)**, jokes about uncertain opening hours. But anyone searching for an unusual gift should make a beeline for this cornucopia of crafts, stocked to the rafters with pots of every description, mirrors, vases, paintings and jewellery. A horse-drawn Wolds waggon, carved with patient skill by an old man of 90, sits in the upstairs window, while downstairs the wonderful fully-clothed Dux (ducks) turn out to be Hoover covers! Standing three feet tall and dressed in Victorian farmhouse garb, you won't want to put them under the stairs!

It was a race against time for young ceramicists Philip Chan and Cathy Abbot to set up their studio at **Betton Farm,** East Ayton **(01723 865100)**, and produce enough to display at the 1994 Birmingham Exhibition. Perhaps invigorated by the Scarborough air, their hard work was rewarded by the Silver Medal for Best Display/Product in the show.

Since then, the pair have been in constant demand, but have resisted approaches by big-name stores. Described by Antiques Roadshow host Eric Knowles as "the antiques of the future", much of their clean and visually simple work is based on the 16th century Japanese firing process known as Raku, with its bright glazes and crazed finish.

South of Scarborough, on the Filey Road, Valerie Green is the fourth generation of the Lazenby family to be an accomplished stained glass artist. Visit **The Stained Glass Centre**, Cayton **(01723 581236)** and you'll see skilled draftsmen carefully drawing the cartoons from which the glass is copied. Though new stained glass panels, mirrors or lampshades can add the finishing touch to your home, restoration occupies much of Valerie's time. Matching the subtler shades of antique glass can be difficult, so Valerie imports much of what she needs from Poland and Russia.

Further north, at Egton near Whitby, iron seems to melt like putty in the hands of wrought ironsmith **James Godbold (01947 895514)**. "If it can be drawn, it can be made" he says, as red hot iron twists and bends under his hammer. James's commissions are impressive and include the restoration of Eaton Hall's famous "Golden Gates" and the entrance to Hartlepool Marina. Elsewhere, in the dungeons of London and Paris, James' medieval torture equipment makes visitors squirm. In the shop adjoining the smithy, wonderful wellie-scrapers, garden furniture, weather vanes and fireside tools are on sale along with traditional toasting forks and chestnut-roasting pans.

On a corner of Whitby's quaint Market Square, the window of olde-worlde **Abbey Gallery (01947 601978)** is filled with brightly coloured candles. Perfumed and floating candles, sculptured and straight, it's a bewildering choice, yet Whitby is famed for only one colour: Jet black.

The luscious, velvety substance, fossilised from the monkey-puzzle wood abundant here in prehistoric times, was much prized by the Victorians. Possessed of the finest jet deposits in the world, the town grew to be a thriving commercial centre. Today, the skills of 19th century artisans are kept alive by only a handful of craftsmen. Their champion is jeweller Hal Redvers Jones, whose beautifully-restored genuine **Victorian Jet Works** on Church Street **(01947 821530)** displays many pieces, both old and new, for sale - alongside fossils and other unusual local finds.

A York jeweller has the honour of owning one of only a handful of Northern galleries selected by the Crafts Council. **Robert Feather (01904 632025)** operates from a combined gallery and workshop on Gillygate - just beyond Bootham Bar. Here can be found the work of over forty of the country's finest contemporary jewellers, plus unusual ceramics, glass and wood. In his own right, Robert Feather is particularly noted for his 18ct gold and platinum rings, whose "understated but effective" designs combine different coloured golds with contrasting polished or textured surfaces.

You'll find unusual ceramics of another kind in the idyllic surroundings of rural Wensleydale. Scan the rooftops around West Burton's lovely village green until you find a cat on a chimney. It marks the famous **Cat Pottery (01969 663273)** where feline companions rule the roost. Aloof or playful, superior or asleep; cats to grace your garden or your home; ready to pounce or prepared to be friendly... they're all here. According to joint proprietor Barrie Nichols, "people love cats, ours go all over the world". With 40 different

felines to chose from, it is surprising to learn that most are modelled from just three animals. The oldest, Chloe, has been a cat-model for 14 years.

En route to Swaledale, call in at **Yorkshire Flowerpots**, Hawes **(01969 667464)** to see Gabriel Nichols and his team up to their elbows in clay. A lot of clay in fact, as much as 5 tons every week! Gabriel makes chimney pots, flower pots, Long Tom pots and wall planters. All are thrown on the potter's wheel before being fired to the high temperature needed to make them frost-proof. Many of Gabriel's classic bell-shaped pots are based on Victorian designs – perfect in the garden or conservatory. Quality seconds are also for sale, making this an ideal stop for even cost-conscious garden lovers.

With grazing sheep at every turn, its no surprise to find that the Swaledale knitting tradition dates from Elizabethan times. By the 1970's the industry was at its lowest ebb, but was saved from extinction by a plan hatched in Muker village pub. Local hand knitters - aged 20 to 90 - combined their skills and resuscitated the craft of knitting warm, durable garments from undyed local wool. **Swaledale Woollens (01748 886251)** is now known world-wide, and counts Arctic explorers and Prince Charles as satisfied customers.

Stef Ottevanger has been making animal models since she was a child. "It was really a self-financing hobby which grew", she explains. Now she exports models of sheep, horses, dogs and other animal characters all over the world. In the studio of **Stef's Models**, Reeth Dales Centre **(01748 884498)**, visitors can watch the entire process through mould-making, casting and hand-painting. Each model is lovingly worked by a dedicated team to give it character and life. A must for souvenir-hunters, the shop stocks a host of enchanting, collectable models made on the premises. Also within the Reeth Dales Centre, furniture maker **Philip Bastow (01748 884555)** takes great care to get the feel for a client's taste and the function of the piece he is making. His pleasure in the grain and pattern of wood translates itself into wonderful furniture. Not only does he make large items, he now fashions a range of attractive smaller items such as mirrors, bowls and incidental tables. He also has a growing reputation for his beautifully-crafted clocks, such as the "Vienna Regulator" which he describes as "his pride and joy".

Leaving the charms of Reeth, take the Barnard Castle road out of the village. On Arkengarthdale Road, opposite a roadside black tin barn, stands **East Windy Hall (01748 884316)**, home and studio of sculptress Joy Bentley, who may well greet you over her stable door. Like latter-day Roman senators, Joy's bronze sculptures are uncanny in their likeness. Among her commissions are strong, rugged-faced men, and children, wide-eyed and smooth cheeked, captured forever in tangible form. Joy's studio is open the first weekend of summer months (2pm to 5pm) or by appointment. She will also be exhibiting during the Swaledale Festival.

Representations of another creature can be found at **Bolly Dolls and Bruin Bears**, Leyburn **(01969 622209)**, where 'real' teddys are made, using the traditional fine mohair fabric and wood wool stuffing, in the workshop of Stella Bolland. Quite different to the modern, floppy creatures made in synthetics and stuffed with something soft, Stella's bears are individuals. "Each has his own name" she explains. "They tell them to us." Certainly, the loveable Oberon, standing nearly two feet tall, is someone to pick up. Tilt him and he growls. His brothers and sisters, who come in many shapes and sizes, have emigrated as far afield as Papua New Guinea. All the components needed to make your own bear are on sale in this charming workshop, and Stella is always pleased to answer questions as she stitches up another furry friend.

Housed in the spacious showrooms of **Wensleydale Picture Framing Gallery** on Leyburn Business Park is the workshop of Simon Fitton. The terrariums **Tana Stained Glass (01969 624864)** originally produced have since been overtaken by commissions for windows and panels in Churches and country houses. Old techniques can be used in modern contexts, and some of Simon's most dramatic work is thoroughly avant garde. His recent life-size female torso, for example. Cleverly made out of tiny pieces of glass and almost sculptural in appearance, it caused quite a stir before going to its home in Florida.

Next door, in the workshop of the **Wensleydale Belt Company (01969 624864)**, join Jayne Stamp and Jasper Pike making strong leather belts, mobile phone holders, pouches and bags. Leathers of different textures and colours are used to good effect and you can stand and watch your own belt being made. Quality products, they are significantly cheaper here than in the shops.

Within the same complex, the secrets of Stradivarius are revealed in **The Violin Making Workshop (01969 624416)**, believed to be the only one of its kind in the country. Essential viewing for music lovers, read about the history of violin making, watch a craftsman at work and enjoy the interactive displays. Maker Roger Hansell is a respected copyist and his instruments, in various stages of being varnished, are always on display. A small shop sells an unusual range of music-related items, books, CDs and giftware.

Around the corner, teapots shaped like Aga cookers, cars and cast iron baths, complete with all fixtures and fittings, will make you smile at the ever-popular **Teapottery (01969 623839)**, whose bizarre products are exported all over the world. Witty and appealing, behind the scenes you'll enjoy watching them being made in the up-to-date pottery before browsing through the seconds and perfect ware in the shop. After you've seen everything, what else can you do but sit down and enjoy the perfect Yorkshire cuppa?

Definitely 'low-tech', a thermostatically-controlled electric dustbin and three bicycle wheels suspended from the ceiling equip Wensley's **White Rose Candles (01969 623544)**. Once an enormous industry, now superseded by electric lighting, candles are still universally enjoyed to create mood and ambience. As you look on, the raw wick is dipped and dried 20 times before yielding the finished product. Beeswax candles, candles in the shape of a pyramid, light bulb or egg are all on show in a splash of colour and wax.

Masham may be small but its brewing reputation is legendary. Though a relative newcomer to Masham's brewing trade, has the expertise of five generations behind it. **The Black Sheep Brewery (01765 689227)** was founded in 1992 by Paul Theakston, who had left T & R Theakston after its 1989 take-over by Scottish & Newcastle. In just a few years, Black Sheep has won acclaim for its three distinct brews, Bitter, Special Bitter and the deep chestnut Riggwelter. Open daily from 10am, the Black Sheep offers a 'shepherded' tour around the traditional brewhouse and fermenting room finishing off in the Black Sheep Baa...r!

Courtesy of T & R Theakston

Dark blue and natural oatmeal colours are the theme at **Masham Pottery & Crafts (01765 689762)**, located in a picturesque stable block behind the King's Head Hotel. Here Howard Charles makes a comprehensive range of robust domestic pottery, decorated with wheat sheaves and sheep, which is ideal for either the kitchen or dining room. Made entirely on the premises, each piece is glazed and made dishwasher, microwave, and oven-proof. Casserole dishes, vases, bread crocks and condiment sets jostle for space with unusual gifts from around the globe in this tasteful, bustling little workshop.

Just a step away, **Uredale Glass (01765 689780)** produces a range of highly col-

lectible glassware from the supremely functional to the purely decorative. Throughout the Easter, Whit and Summer holidays glass-blowing demonstrations are held five times a day (Tuesday to Saturday), with an informative commentary and plenty of opportunity to ask questions. In the showroom, alongside their distinctive range of vases, goblets and bowls, you'll also find a selection of larger 'one-off' pieces signed by the maker.

If you're looking for a wedding or engagement ring that is just a little different, why not call in on **Delyth St John Lewis (01765 689833)** close by. Distinctively set with precious stones, her rings use coloured golds with different textures and finishes for maximum effect. The Masham Rose Collection is a unique range of sterling silver jewellery based on the Yorkshire Rose. Reasonably-priced cufflinks, earrings, pendants and charms offer a perfect souvenir of this compact Dales town.

Just outside the town, you'll relish a trip to **Rosebud Preserves (01765 689174)** which occupies a converted barn in Healey. Wild fruit jellies such as crabapple or rowan and spicy chutneys vie for your attention among its range of products. Created using only the finest ingredients and packed with chunky pieces of real fruit, Rosebud preserves are every bit as good as home-made. Stocked by Harvey Nichols and famous locally, their delicious products may tempt you to put away the jam pan forever!

Another of the most popular tourist attractions in the Yorkshire Dales, the Visitor Centre at the nearby **T & R Theakston Brewery (01765 689057)** welcomed 25,000 visitors in 1996. The dying art of cooperage (making wooden casks for ale) can be viewed here, as Theakstons employ two of Britain's seven remaining working coopers. The brewing process is explained through multimedia displays and enthusiasts will enjoy the brewery tour which is also available. Flat shoes and good health are paramount, as the brewery's ancient nooks and crannies are quite challenging.

Similar principles but different ingredients are used by **Yorkshire Country Wines**, Glasshouses **(01423 711947)**, whose proprietors can often be spotted scouring the hedgerows for elderflower and dandelions during the summer months. Their hard work is well worth it, for the resulting country wines produced in the vaulted cellars of their 19th century Flax Mill are quite delicious. Elderberry, at 13%, is the most alcoholic, but parsnip and gooseberry and many other lighter wines are all available for tasting. Less heady beverages are available in the Tearoom. A former Steam Engine Room, it has been tastefully converted to provide idyllic views of the River Nidd.

In elegant Harrogate, close to Betty's Tearooms, lovers of handicrafts will find a brand new specialist centre for needlepoint, cross-stitch and embroidery. Overlooking the Stray on Montpellier Parade, **Petit Point's (01423 565632)** spacious premises are notable for their relaxed atmosphere and attractive, uncluttered surroundings. A pleasure to shop in, unobtrusive assistance from knowledgeable staff make this family-owned and managed store excellent for beginners and experts alike.

Sponsored by T. & R. Theakston.

THE WORLD OF W
HARDRAW FORCE
Highest fall of unbroken water in Yorkshire.
CASTLE BOLTON
Village taking its name from Bolton Castle, seat of the Scrope family where Mary, Queen of Scots, was once a prisoner.
ASKRIGG
Substantial grey-stone village made famous throug the T.V. 'Herriot' series. Cheese was made here until the war years.
HAWES
Hawes has long been a focal point for trade and tourism.
Home of Kit Calvert, 'King of Wensleydale Cheese'. One of two creameries associated with Kit, Wensleydale Products, is situated between Hawes and Gayle.
AYSGARTH
Famed for its series of fine waterfalls.
COVERDALE
Traditional Coverdale Cheese is still made uniquely at Fountains Dairies, Kirkby Malzeard, where it was reintroduced after 50 years.
SEMERWATER
One of the very few natural lakes in Yorkshire. According to legend its waters cover a submerged city, cursed for refusing hospitality.
KIT CALVERT
Born in the village of Burtersett the legendary Kit Calvert was the archetypal dalesman, often seen smoking his clay pipe. Starting as a dairy farmer he became the architect of the Wensleydale Cheese industry, saving many creameries and building them into a successful group. This was bought by the Milk Marketing Board who closed all the small dairies, leaving two main creameries at Hawes and Kirkby Malzeard, the latter acting as the headquarters under Kit's successor, Bill Taylor.
Peter Kearney
1997
Map and illustrations by Peter Kearney
Text by A

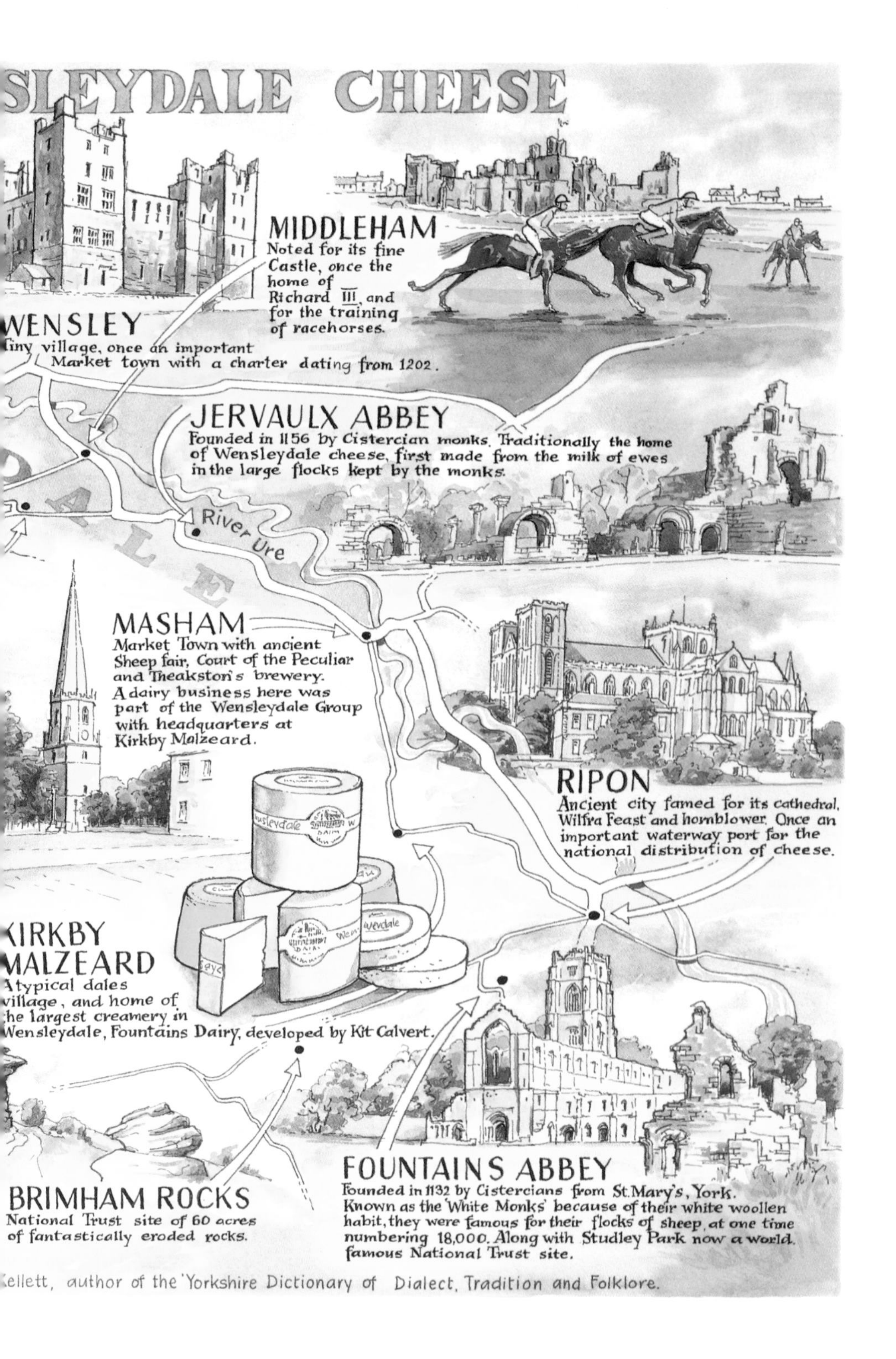

ellett, author of the 'Yorkshire Dictionary of Dialect, Tradition and Folklore.

Courses for Horses

Standing proudly on the slopes of Wensleydale, the royal and ancient town of Middleham is surely a must for any first time visitor remotely interested in either horses or history.

Although proud of its long and distinguished past, Middleham has ensured its own prosperity by actively promoting the thriving local racehorse industry – responsible for over five hundred thoroughbreds housed in fifteen training yards situated in and around the town.

Morning Gallops

Morning is undoubtedly the best time to see Middleham. Visitors are advised to step lively on the town's part-cobbled pavements – it's all hustle and bustle as long lines of smartly turned out racehorses trot purposefully by, heading for the nearby Low Moor gallops.

And if you get your skates on, you can follow them up the winding hill out of Middleham and onto the moor itself – then watch from the sidelines as horse and rider stretch out on the miles of open grassland ahead.

Spectacular Views

If the bracing moorland wind does not take your breath away, the spectacular views of both Coverdale and Wensleydale almost certainly will. And if all this fails to get the adrenalin pumping, the sight of racehorses blazing up the gallops at full pelt might still send a shiver down your spine.

High Moor

For horse racing devotees, the short two mile drive up to Middleham's other training ground, the High Moor, should not be missed. It was on this very turf back in the mid 18th century that the seeds of the presently flourishing industry were sown.

Existing records suggest Isaac Cape (1720-1789) was the first professional trainer to be installed in the area. He used the unique mile-and-half horseshoe shaped grass gallops on High Moor to help his horses attain peak fitness. Other trainers soon followed suit giving rise to an official racecourse on the Moor (circa 1750-1873). A small set of stables, known as the "Rubbing Houses", survive to this day, and it is planned to convert them into a visitor information centre in the near future.

All-Weather Gallop

They say the best things in life are free, and there is no charge to gallop-watchers on High Moor, where, believe it or not, the views even surpass those already described from Low Moor. Although the grass gallops are only used during the summer months, the recent installation of a superb all-weather man-made gallop means the racehorses can exercise for virtually 365 days a year. The project, completed in late 1996, was funded by the Middleham Key Partnership, sponsored by the Rural Development Commission in association with the Middleham Trainers Association, at a cost of £250,000.

Champions

Many many champion racehorses have graced the turf on both Middleham's High and Low Moors. Grand National winners, Derby, Oaks and St Leger winners, and most recently, Mister Baileys, who triumphed for top local trainer Mark Johnston in the 1994 2000 Guineas. Other recent stars include Ascot Gold Cup winner Double Trigger, who is virtually a household name these days, plus Cheltenham Festival winners Paddy's Return and Stop The Waller.

Courtesy of Zillah Bell

Stable Visits

Primarily for safety reasons, training stables are not normally open to the public. However, most trainers are happy for their respective yards to be visited by prior arrangement. Chairman of the Middleham Trainer's Association, Chris Thornton, has all the details and can be contacted at Spigot Lodge, Middleham, telephone 01969 623350.

Middleham Castle

A trip to Wensleydale would not be complete without a visit to historic Middleham Castle. Although over eight hundred years have elapsed since building began in 1170, much of the huge castle remains intact. In its heyday the castle was home to Richard III, who briefly ruled England from Middleham during the period 1483-1485. The town was dubbed "The Windsor of the North", and although its period of major historical significance was confined to a relatively short space of time, relics of the castle's fascinating past are still being discovered today.

Admission and opening times: Open April to September 10am to 6pm. October 10am to 4pm. November to March 1997 10pm to 4pm (closed Monday and Tuesday). Adults £1.60, children 80p

The Middleham Jewel

As recently as 1985 a fabulous gold pendant was unearthed close to the castle's immaculately kept grounds. Labelled by the world-wide media as the "Middleham Jewel", it was subsequently sold by Sotheby's in London, the auctioneer's hammer finally crashing down at the astonishing sum of 1.3 million pounds.

Jervaulx Abbey

Middleham most likely owes a lot of its current prosperity to nearby Jervaulx Abbey. Built in the 12th century and occupied for the following 400 years by an order of French Cistercian Monks, the haunting ruins can be seen to this day. The monks were renowned horse breeders, probably setting up the first established equine trading centre in the area. Legend also tells us that the monks were the first to make the now world-famous Wensleydale cheese. Nowadays, there is an attractive visitor centre across the road from the Abbey, incorporating a gift shop and country tea room.

Admission and opening times: Open every day. Adults £1.50, children £1, payable at the visitor centre, or in the honesty box at the Abbey.

YORKSHIRE RACECOURSES

Please note (e) denotes evening meeting.

Catterick

Handily placed just off the A1, Catterick's all-year-round programme of Flat and Jump racing means the next fixture is never far away. The tight oval circuit ensures punters stay close to the action at all times. For the kids there is a free children's playground in the central course enclosure.

Admission: Tattersalls £7. Course Enclosure £2.50. Accompanied children (under 16) free. Free parking.

Fixtures: Flat: May 30, 31. June 6. July 3, 16, 23. August 5, 15(e). September 20, 27. October 16, 17. National Hunt: November 22, 24. December 3, 17, 18, 31.

Ripon

Known as "Yorkshire's Garden Racecourse", few can match Ripon's picturesque setting and floral displays. Racegoers will not be disappointed either with the admirable standard of Flat racing, plus numerous bars and restaurants. A fully staffed creche is available from half an hour before the first race until half and hour after the last race. Unsupervised children's playgrounds are also available in the Silver Ring and Course Enclosures.

Admission: Tattersalls: £8, Silver Ring £4, Course Enclosure £2.50 (Car on course £8, max 4 persons).

Fixtures: May 18, 28(e). June 18(e), 19. July 7(e), 19. August 4, 16, 25, 26, 30.

Thirsk

Thirsk combines excellent Flat racing with superb family facilities. Well-manicured lawns and beautifully-planted flowerbeds make the paddock area one of the most attractive in the country. Alternatively, the competitively-priced Family Ring makes a great day out for children and picnics. Good disabled facilities.

Admission prices: Tattersalls £8. Family ring: Adults £3, accompanied children (under 16) free. There is also access for cars to the Family Ring, inc. up to 4 adults for £9. All OAPs half price. Free parking.

Fixtures: May 3, 16, 17. June 2(e), 17. July 25. August 1, 2, 11(e), 22. September 6.

Beverley

Horse racing has taken place at Beverley since 1690. So steeped is the area in equine tradition, that it comes as no surprise to see the sport remaining popular in the town to this day, especially with such a well-appointed racecourse on its doorstep. Not only do the superbly positioned stands provide an excellent all round view of the course, but also a clear sight of Beverley's magnificent ancient Minster. The family picnic area is right by the winning post, so everyone gets a real close-up of the action.

Admission: Tattersalls £8 (OAPs £6), Silver Ring £3 (OAPs £2), Family Ring £2 per car plus £2 per person, accompanied children under 16 free. Disabled facilities are excellent at this course.

Fixtures: May 10, 11 (Sunday meeting – all rings £5), 20. June 4(e), 5, 11. July 4(e), 5, 15, 21(e), 29. August 13, 14, 23. September 17.

Redcar

When the sun shines at Redcar, it really is the ideal venue for both the family and serious racegoer. The town, very much in the mould of a traditional holiday resort, boasts a long sandy beach – a must for the youngsters. For racing fans, the two-mile galloping racecourse seems always to attract top thoroughbreds from Newmarket and Lambourn in the south, plus Middleham and Malton in the north.

Admission: Tattersalls £8 (OAPs £3.50).